MW01141067

Credit Cards: Increased Complexity in Rates and Fees Heightens Need for More Effective Disclosures to Consumers

United States Government Accountability Office

The BiblioGov Project is an effort to expand awareness of the public documents and records of the U.S. Government via print publications. In broadening the public understanding of government and its work, an enlightened democracy can grow and prosper. Ranging from historic Congressional Bills to the most recent Budget of the United States Government, the BiblioGov Project spans a wealth of government information. These works are now made available through an environmentally friendly, print-on-demand basis, using only what is necessary to meet the required demands of an interested public. We invite you to learn of the records of the U.S. Government, heightening the knowledge and debate that can lead from such publications.

Included are the following Collections:

Budget of The United States Government
Presidential Documents
United States Code
Education Reports from ERIC
GAO Reports
History of Bills
House Rules and Manual
Public and Private Laws

Code of Federal Regulations
Congressional Documents
Economic Indicators
Federal Register
Government Manuals
House Journal
Privacy act Issuances
Statutes at Large

United States Government Accountability Office

GAO

Report to the Ranking Minority Member, Permanent Subcommittee on Investigations, Committee on Homeland Security and Governmental Affairs, U.S. Senate

September 2006

CREDIT CARDS

Increased Complexity in Rates and Fees Heightens Need for More Effective Disclosures to Consumers

GAO
Accountability ★ Integrity ★ Reliability

GAO-06-929

Highlights of GAO-06-929, a report to the Ranking Minority Member, Permanent Subcommittee on Investigations, Committee on Homeland Security and Governmental Affairs, U.S. Senate

CREDIT CARDS

Increased Complexity in Rates and Fees Heightens Need for More Effective Disclosures to Consumers

Why GAO Did This Study

With credit card penalty rates and fees now common, the Federal Reserve has begun efforts to revise disclosures to better inform consumers of these costs. Questions have also been raised about the relationship among penalty charges, consumer bankruptcies, and issuer profits. GAO examined (1) how card fees and other practices have evolved and how cardholders have been affected, (2) how effectively these pricing practices are disclosed to cardholders, (3) the extent to which penalty charges contribute to cardholder bankruptcies, and (4) card issuers' revenues and profitability. Among other things, GAO analyzed disclosures from popular cards; obtained data on rates and fees paid on cardholder accounts from 6 large issuers; employed a usability consultant to analyze and test disclosures; interviewed a sample of consumers selected to represent a range of education and income levels; and analyzed academic and regulatory studies on bankruptcy and card issuer revenues.

What GAO Recommends

As part of revising card disclosures, the Federal Reserve should ensure that such disclosure materials more clearly emphasize those terms that can significantly affect cardholder costs, such as the actions that can cause default or other penalty pricing rates to be imposed. The Federal Reserve generally concurred with the report.

www.gao.gov/cgi-bin/getrpt?GAO-06-929.

To view the full product, including the scope and methodology, click on the link above. For more information, contact David G. Wood at (202) 512-8678 or woodd@gao.gov.

What GAO Found

Originally having fixed interest rates around 20 percent and few fees, popular credit cards now feature a variety of interest rates and other fees, including penalties for making late payments that have increased to as high as $39 per occurrence and interest rates of over 30 percent for cardholders who pay late or exceed a credit limit. Issuers explained that these practices represent risk-based pricing that allows them to offer cards with lower costs to less risky cardholders while providing cards to riskier consumers who might otherwise be unable to obtain such credit. Although costs can vary significantly, many cardholders now appear to have cards with lower interest rates than those offered in the past; data from the top six issuers reported to GAO indicate that, in 2005, about 80 percent of their accounts were assessed interest rates of less than 20 percent, with over 40 percent having rates below 15 percent. The issuers also reported that 35 percent of their active U.S. accounts were assessed late fees and 13 percent were assessed over-limit fees in 2005.

Although issuers must disclose information intended to help consumers compare card costs, disclosures by the largest issuers have various weaknesses that reduced consumers' ability to use and understand them. According to a usability expert's review, disclosures from the largest credit card issuers were often written well above the eighth-grade level at which about half of U.S. adults read. Contrary to usability and readability best practices, the disclosures buried important information in text, failed to group and label related material, and used small typefaces. Perhaps as a result, cardholders that the expert tested often had difficulty using the disclosures to find and understand key rates or terms applicable to the cards. Similarly, GAO's interviews with 112 cardholders indicated that many failed to understand key aspects of their cards, including when they would be charged for late payments or what actions could cause issuers to raise rates. These weaknesses may arise from issuers drafting disclosures to avoid lawsuits, and from federal regulations that highlight less relevant information and are not well suited for presenting the complex rates or terms that cards currently feature. Although the Federal Reserve has started to obtain consumer input, its staff recognizes the challenge of designing disclosures that include all key information in a clear manner.

Although penalty charges reduce the funds available to repay cardholders' debts, their role in contributing to bankruptcies was not clear. The six largest issuers reported that unpaid interest and fees represented about 10 percent of the balances owed by bankrupt cardholders, but were unable to provide data on penalty charges these cardholders paid prior to filing for bankruptcy. Although revenues from penalty interest and fees have increased, profits of the largest issuers have been stable in recent years. GAO analysis indicates that while the majority of issuer revenues came from interest charges, the portion attributable to penalty rates has grown.

Contents

Letter

1

Results in Brief	4
Background	9
Credit Card Fees and Issuer Practices That Can Increase Cardholder Costs Have Expanded, but a Minority of Cardholders Appear to Be Affected	13
Weaknesses in Credit Card Disclosures Appear to Hinder Cardholder Understanding of Fees and Other Practices That Can Affect Their Costs	33
Although Credit Card Penalty Fees and Interest Could Increase Indebtedness, the Extent to Which They Have Contributed to Bankruptcies Was Unclear	56
Although Penalty Interest and Fees Likely Have Grown as a Share of Credit Card Revenues, Large Card Issuers' Profitability Has Been Stable	67
Conclusions	77
Recommendation for Executive Action	79
Agency Comments and Our Evaluation	79

Appendixes

Appendix I:	Objectives, Scope and Methodology	81
Appendix II:	Consumer Bankruptcies Have Risen Along with Debt	86
Appendix III:	Factors Contributing to the Profitability of Credit Card Issuers	96
Appendix IV:	Comments from the Federal Reserve Board	106
Appendix V:	GAO Contact and Staff Acknowledgments	108

Tables

Table 1:	Various Fees for Services and Transactions, Charged in 2005 on Popular Large-Issuer Cards	23
Table 2:	Portion of Credit Card Debt Held by Households	93
Table 3:	Credit Card Debt Balances Held by Household Income	93
Table 4:	Revenues and Profits of Credit Card Issuers in Card Industry Directory per $100 of Credit Card Assets	104

Figures

Figure 1:	Credit Cards in Use and Charge Volume, 1980-2005	10
Figure 2:	The 10 Largest Credit Card Issuers by Credit Card Balances Outstanding as of December 31, 2004	11
Figure 3:	Credit Card Interest Rates, 1972-2005	16

Figure 4:   Average Annual Late Fees Reported from Issuer Surveys,
            1995-2005 (unadjusted for inflation)   19
Figure 5:   Average Annual Over-limit fees Reported from Issuer
            Surveys, 1995-2005 (unadjusted for inflation)   21
Figure 6:   How the Double-Cycle Billing Method Works   28
Figure 7:   Example of Important Information Not Prominently
            Presented in Typical Credit Card Disclosure
            Documents   39
Figure 8:   Example of How Related Information Was Not Being
            Grouped Together in Typical Credit Card Disclosure
            Documents   40
Figure 9:   Example of How Use of Small Font Sizes Reduces
            Readability in Typical Credit Card Disclosure
            Documents   42
Figure 10: Example of How Use of Ineffective Font Types Reduces
            Readability in Typical Credit Card Disclosure
            Documents   43
Figure 11: Example of How Use of Inappropriate Emphasis Reduces
            Readability in Typical Credit Card Disclosure
            Documents   43
Figure 12: Example of Ineffective and Effective Use of Headings in
            Typical Credit Card Disclosure Documents   44
Figure 13: Example of How Presentation Techniques Can Affect
            Readability in Typical Credit Card Disclosure
            Documents   46
Figure 14: Examples of How Removing Overly Complex Language
            Can Improve Readability in Typical Credit Card
            Disclosure Documents   47
Figure 15: Example of Superfluous Detail in Typical Credit Card
            Disclosure Documents   48
Figure 16: Hypothetical Impact of Penalty Interest and Fee Charges
            on Two Cardholders   63
Figure 17: Example of a Typical Bank's Income Statement   70
Figure 18: Proportion of Active Accounts of the Six Largest Card
            Issuers with Various Interest Rates for Purchases, 2003 to
            2005   71
Figure 19: Example of a Typical Credit Card Purchase Transaction
            Showing How Interchange Fees Paid by Merchants Are
            Allocated   74
Figure 20: Average Pretax Return on Assets for Large Credit Card
            Banks and All Commercial Banks, 1986 to 2004   76
Figure 21: U.S. Consumer Bankruptcy Filings, 1980-2005   86

Figure 22: U.S. Household Debt, 1980-2005   87
Figure 23: Credit Card and Other Revolving and Nonrevolving Debt
           Outstanding, 1990 to 2005   89
Figure 24: Percent of Households Holding Credit Card Debt by
           Household Income, 1998, 2001, and 2004   90
Figure 25: U.S. Household Debt Burden and Financial Obligations
           Ratios, 1980 to 2005   92
Figure 26: Households Reporting Financial Distress by Household
           Income, 1995 through 2004   94
Figure 27: Average Credit Card, Car Loans and Personal Loan
           Interest Rates   97
Figure 28: Net Interest Margin for Credit Card Issuers and Other
           Consumer Lenders in 2005   98
Figure 29: Charge-off Rates for Credit Card and Other Consumer
           Lenders, 2004 to 2005   99
Figure 30: Charge-off Rates for the Top 5 Credit Card Issuers, 2003
           to 2005   100
Figure 31: Operating Expense as Percentage of Total Assets for
           Various Types of Lenders in 2005   101
Figure 32: Non-Interest Revenue as Percentage of Their Assets for
           Card Lenders and Other Consumer Lenders   102
Figure 33: Net Interest Margin for All Banks Focusing on Credit
           Card Lending, 1987-2005   103

Abbreviations

APR	Annual Percentage Rate
FDIC	Federal Deposit Insurance Corporation
OCC	Office of the Comptroller of the Currency
ROA	Return on assets
SEC	Securities and Exchange Commission
TILA	Truth in Lending Act

United States Government Accountability Office
Washington, D.C. 20548

September 12, 2006

The Honorable Carl Levin
Ranking Minority Member
Permanent Subcommittee on Investigations
Committee on Homeland Security and Governmental Affairs
United States Senate

Dear Senator Levin:

Over the past 25 years, the prevalence and use of credit cards in the United States has grown dramatically. Between 1980 and 2005, the amount that U.S. consumers charged to their cards grew from an estimated $69 billion per year to more than $1.8 trillion, according to one firm that analyzes the card industry.[1] This firm also reports that the number of U.S. credit cards issued to consumers now exceeds 691 million. The increased use of credit cards has contributed to an expansion in household debt, which grew from $59 billion in 1980 to roughly $830 billion by the end of 2005.[2] The Board of Governors of the Federal Reserve System (Federal Reserve) estimates that in 2004, the average American household owed about $2,200 in credit card debt, up from about $1,000 in 1992.[3]

Generally, a consumer's cost of using a credit card is determined by the terms and conditions applicable to the card—such as the interest rate(s), minimum payment amounts, and payment schedules, which are typically presented in a written cardmember agreement—and how a consumer uses

---

[1]CardWeb.com, Inc., an online publisher of information about the payment card industry.

[2]Based on data from the Federal Reserve Board's monthly G.19 release on consumer credit. In addition to credit card debt, the Federal Reserve also categorizes overdraft lines of credit as revolving consumer debt (an overdraft line of credit is a loan a consumer obtains from a bank to cover the amount of potential overdrafts or withdrawals from a checking account in amounts greater than the balance available in the account). Mortgage debt is not captured in these data.

[3]B.K. Bucks, A.B. Kennickell, and K.B. Moore, "Recent Changes in U.S. Family Finances: Evidence from the 2001 and 2004 Survey of Consumer Finances," *Federal Reserve Bulletin*, March 22, 2006. Also, A.B. Kennickell and M. Starr-McCluer, "Changes in Family Finances from 1989 to 1992: Evidence from the Survey of Consumer Finances," *Federal Reserve Bulletin*, October 1994. Adjusted for inflation, credit card debt in 1992 was $1,298 for the average American household.

a card.[4] The Federal Reserve, under the Truth in Lending Act (TILA), is responsible for creating and enforcing requirements relating to the disclosure of terms and conditions of consumer credit, including those applicable to credit cards.[5] The regulation that implements TILA's requirements is the Federal Reserve's Regulation Z.[6] As credit card use and debt have grown, representatives of consumer groups and issuers have questioned the extent to which consumers understand their credit card terms and conditions, including issuers' practices that—even if permitted under applicable terms and conditions—could increase consumers' costs of using credit cards. These practices include the application of fees or relatively high penalty interest rates if cardholders pay late or exceed credit limits. Issuers also can allocate customers' payments among different components of their outstanding balances in ways that maximize total interest charges. Although card issuers have argued that these practices are appropriate because they compensate for the greater risks posed by cardholders who make late payments or exhibit other risky behaviors, consumer groups say that the fees and practices are harmful to the financial condition of many cardholders and that card issuers use them to generate profits.

You requested that we review a number of issues related to credit card fees and practices, specifically of the largest issuers of credit cards in the United States. This report discusses (1) how the interest, fees, and other practices that affect the pricing structure of cards from the largest U.S. issuers have evolved and cardholders' experiences under these pricing structures in recent years; (2) how effectively the issuers disclose the pricing structures of cards to their cardholders (3) whether credit card debt and penalty interest and fees contribute to cardholder bankruptcies; and (4) the extent to which penalty interest and fees contribute to the revenues and profitability of issuers' credit card operations.

To identify the pricing structures of cards—including their interest rates, fees, and other practices—we analyzed the cardmember agreements, as

---

[4]We recently reported on minimum payment disclosure requirements. See GAO, *Credit Cards: Customized Minimum Payment Disclosures Would Provide More Information to Consumers, but Impact Could Vary*, GAO-06-434 (Washington, D.C.: Apr. 21, 2006).

[5]Pub. L. No. 90-321, Title I, 82 Stat. 146 (1968) (codified as amended at 15 U.S.C. §§ 1601-1666).

[6]Regulation Z is codified at 12 C.F.R. Part 226.

well as materials used by the six largest issuers as of December 31, 2004, for 28 popular cards used to solicit new credit card customers from 2003 through 2005.[7] To determine the extent to which these issuers' cardholders were assessed interest and fees, we obtained data from each of the six largest issuers about their cardholder accounts and their operations. To protect each issuer's proprietary information, a third-party organization, engaged by counsel to the issuers, aggregated these data and then provided the results to us. Although the six largest issuers whose accounts were included in this survey and whose cards we reviewed may include some subprime accounts, we did not include information in this report relating to cards offered by credit card issuers that engage primarily in subprime lending.[8] To assess the effectiveness of the disclosures that issuers provide to cardholders in terms of their usability or readability, we contracted with a consulting firm that specializes in assessing the readability and usability of written and other materials to analyze a representative selection of the largest issuers' cardmember agreements and solicitation materials, including direct mail applications and letters, used for opening an account (in total, the solicitation materials for four cards and cardmember agreements for the same four cards).[9] The consulting firm compared these materials to recognized industry guidelines for readability and presentation and conducted testing to assess how well cardholders could use the materials to identify and understand information about these credit cards. While the materials used for the readability and usability assessments appeared to be typical of the large issuers' disclosures, the results cannot be generalized to materials that were not reviewed. We also conducted structured interviews to learn about the card-using behavior and knowledge of various credit card terms and conditions of 112 consumers recruited by a market research organization to represent a range of adult income and education levels. However, our sample of cardholders was too

---

[7]These issuers' accounts constitute almost 80 percent of credit card lending in the United States. Participating issuers were Citibank (South Dakota), N.A.; Chase Bank USA, N.A.; Bank of America; MBNA America Bank, N.A.; Capital One Bank; and Discover Financial Services. In providing us with materials for the most popular credit cards, these issuers determined which of their cards qualified as popular among all cards in their portfolios.

[8]Subprime lending generally refers to extending credit to borrowers who exhibit characteristics indicating a significantly higher risk of default than traditional bank lending customers. Such issuers could have pricing structures and other terms significantly different from those of the popular cards offered by the top issuers.

[9]Regulation Z defines a "solicitation" as an offer (written or oral) by the card issuer to open a credit or charge card account that does not require the consumer to complete an application. 12 C.F.R. § 226.5a(a)(1).

small to be statistically representative of all cardholders, thus the results of our interviews cannot be generalized to the population of all U.S. cardholders. We also reviewed comment letters submitted to the Federal Reserve in response to its comprehensive review of Regulation Z's open-end credit rules, including rules pertaining to credit card disclosures.[10] To determine the extent to which credit card debt and penalty interest and fees contributed to cardholder bankruptcies, we analyzed studies, reports, and bank regulatory data relating to credit card debt and consumer bankruptcies, as well as information reported to us as part of the data request to the six largest issuers. To determine the extent to which penalty interest and fees contributes to card issuers' revenues and profitability, we analyzed publicly available sources of revenue and profitability data for card issuers, including information included in reports filed with the Securities and Exchange Commission and bank regulatory reports, in addition to information reported to us as part of the data request to the six largest issuers.[11] In addition, we spoke with representatives of other U.S. banks that are large credit card issuers, as well as representatives of consumer groups, industry associations, academics, organizations that collect and analyze information on the credit card industry, and federal banking regulators. We also reviewed research reports and academic studies of the credit card industry.

We conducted our work from June 2005 to September 2006 in Boston; Chicago; Charlotte, North Carolina; New York City; San Francisco; Wilmington, Delaware; and Washington, D.C., in accordance with generally accepted government auditing standards. Appendix I describes the objectives, scope, and methodology of our review in more detail.

Results in Brief

Since about 1990, the pricing structures of credit cards have evolved to encompass a greater variety of interest rates and fees that can increase

---

[10]See Truth in Lending, 69 Fed. Reg. 70925 (advanced notice of proposed rulemaking, published Dec. 8, 2004). "Open-end credit" means consumer credit extended by a creditor under a plan in which: (i) the creditor reasonably contemplates repeated transactions, (ii) the creditor may impose a finance charge from time to time on an outstanding unpaid balance and (iii) the amount of credit that may be extended to the consumer is generally made available to the extent that any outstanding balance is repaid. 12 C.F.R. § 226.2(a)(20).

[11]Although we had previously been provided comprehensive data from Visa International on credit industry revenues and profits for a past report on credit card issues, we were unable to obtain these data for this report.

cardholder's costs; however, cardholders generally are assessed lower interest rates than those that prevailed in the past, and most have not been assessed penalty fees. For many years after being introduced, credit cards generally charged fixed single rates of interest of around 20 percent, had few fees, and were offered only to consumers with high credit standing. After 1990, card issuers began to introduce cards with a greater variety of interest rates and fees, and the amounts that cardholders can be charged have been growing. For example, our analysis of 28 popular cards and other information indicates that cardholders could be charged

- up to three different interest rates for different transactions, such as one rate for purchases and another for cash advances, with rates for purchases that ranged from about 8 percent to about 19 percent;

- penalty fees for certain cardholder actions, such as making a late payment (an average of almost $34 in 2005, up from an average of about $13 in 1995) or exceeding a credit limit (an average of about $31 in 2005, up from about $13 in 1995); and

- a higher interest rate—some charging over 30 percent—as a penalty for exhibiting riskier behavior, such as paying late.

Although consumer groups and others have criticized these fees and other practices, issuers point out that the costs to use a card can now vary according to the risk posed by the cardholder, which allows issuers to offer credit with lower costs to less-risky cardholders and credit to consumers with lower credit standing, who likely would have not have received a credit card in the past. Although cardholder costs can vary significantly in this new environment, many cardholders now appear to have cards with interest rates less than the 20 percent rate that most cards charged prior to 1990. Data reported by the top six issuers indicate that, in 2005, about 80 percent of their active U.S. accounts were assessed interest rates of less than 20 percent—with more than 40 percent having rates of 15 percent or less.[12] Furthermore, almost half of the active accounts paid little or no interest because the cardholder generally paid the balance in full. The issuers also reported that, in 2005, 35 percent of their active U.S. accounts were assessed late fees and 13 percent were assessed over-limit fees.

---

[12]For purposes of this report, active accounts refer to accounts of the top six issuers that had had a debit or credit posted to them by December 31 in 2003, 2004, and 2005.

Although credit card issuers are required to provide cardholders with information aimed at facilitating informed use of credit and enhancing consumers' ability to compare the costs and terms of credit, we found that these disclosures have serious weaknesses that likely reduced consumers' ability to understand the costs of using credit cards. Because the pricing of credit cards, including interest rates and fees, is not generally subject to federal regulation, the disclosures required under TILA and Regulation Z are the primary means under federal law for protecting consumers against inaccurate and unfair credit card practices.[13] However, the assessment by our usability consultant found that the disclosures in the customer solicitation materials and cardmember agreements provided by four of the largest credit card issuers were too complicated for many consumers to understand. For example, although about half of adults in the United States read at or below the eighth-grade level, most of the credit card materials were written at a tenth- to twelfth-grade level. In addition, the required disclosures often were poorly organized, burying important information in text or scattering information about a single topic in numerous places. The design of the disclosures often made them hard to read, with large amounts of text in small, condensed typefaces and poor, ineffective headings to distinguish important topics from the surrounding text. Perhaps as a result of these weaknesses, the cardholders tested by the consultant often had difficulty using these disclosures to locate and understand key rates or terms applicable to the cards. Similarly, our interviews with 112 cardholders indicated that many failed to understand key terms or conditions that could affect their costs, including when they would be charged for late payments or what actions could cause issuers to raise rates. The disclosure materials that consumers found so difficult to use resulted from issuers' attempts to reduce regulatory and liability exposure by adhering to the formats and language prescribed by federal law and regulations, which no longer suit the complex features and terms of many cards. For example, current disclosures require that less important terms, such as minimum finance charge or balance computation method, be prominently disclosed, whereas information that could more significantly affect consumers' costs, such as the actions that could raise their interest rate, are not as prominently disclosed. With the goal of improving credit card disclosures, the Federal Reserve has begun obtaining public and industry input as part of a comprehensive review of Regulation Z. Industry participants and others have provided various suggestions to improve

---

[13]TILA also contains procedural and substantive protections for consumers for credit card transactions.

disclosures, such as placing all key terms in one brief document and other details in a much longer separate document, and both our work and that of others illustrated that involving consultants and consumers can help develop disclosure materials that are more likely to be effective. Federal Reserve staff told us that they have begun to involve consumers in the preparation of potentially new and revised disclosures. Nonetheless, Federal Reserve staff recognize the challenge of presenting the variety of information that consumers may need to understand the costs of their cards in a clear way, given the complexity of credit card products and the different ways in which consumers use credit cards.

Although paying penalty interest and fees can slow cardholders' attempts to reduce their debt, the extent to which credit card penalty fees and interest have contributed to consumer bankruptcies is unclear. The number of consumers filing for bankruptcy has risen more than sixfold over the past 25 years—a period when the nation's population grew by 29 percent—to more than 2 million filings in 2005, but debate continues over the reasons for this increase. Some researchers attribute the rise in bankruptcies to the significant increase in household debt levels that also occurred over this period, including the dramatic increase in outstanding credit card debt. However, others have found that relatively steady household debt burden ratios over the last 15 years indicate that the ability of households to make payments on this expanded indebtedness has kept pace with growth in their incomes. Similarly, the percentage of households that appear to be in financial distress—those with debt payments that exceed 40 percent of their income—did not change much during this period, nor did the proportion of lower-income households with credit card balances. Because debt levels alone did not appear to clearly explain the rise in bankruptcies, some researchers instead cited other explanations, such as a general decline in the stigma associated with bankruptcies or the increased costs of major life events—such as health problems or divorce—to households that increasingly rely on two incomes. Although critics of the credit card industry have cited the emergence of penalty interest rates and growth in fees as leading to increased financial distress, no comprehensive data exist to determine the extent to which these charges contributed to consumer bankruptcies. Any penalty charges that cardholders pay would consume funds that could have been used to repay principal, and we obtained anecdotal information on a few court cases involving consumers who incurred sizable penalty charges that contributed to their financial distress. However, credit card issuers said that they have little incentive to cause their customers to go bankrupt. The six largest issuers reported to us that of their active accounts in 2005 pertaining to cardholders who had filed for bankruptcy before their account became 6 months delinquent, about 10 percent of the outstanding balances on those accounts represented unpaid interest and fees. However, issuers told us that their data system and recordkeeping limitations prevented them from providing us with data that would more completely illustrate a relationship between penalty charges and bankruptcies, such as the amount of penalty charges that bankrupt cardholders paid in the months prior to filing for bankruptcy or the amount of penalty charges owed by cardholders who went bankrupt after their accounts became more than 6 months delinquent.

Although penalty interest and fees have likely increased as a portion of issuer revenues, the largest issuers have not experienced greatly increased profitability over the last 20 years. Determining the extent to which penalty interest charges and fees contribute to issuers' revenues and profits was difficult because issuers' regulatory filings and other public sources do not include such detail. Using data from bank regulators, industry analysts, and information reported by the five largest issuers, we estimate that the majority—about 70 percent in recent years—of issuer revenues came from interest charges, and the portion attributable to penalty rates appears to have been growing. The remaining issuer revenues came from penalty fees—which had generally grown and were estimated to represent around 10 percent of total issuer revenues—as well as fees that issuers receive for processing merchants' card transactions and other sources. The profits of the largest credit-card-issuing banks, which are generally the most profitable group of lenders, have generally been stable over the last 7 years.

This report recommends that, as part of its effort to increase the effectiveness of disclosure materials, the Federal Reserve should ensure that such disclosures, including model forms and formatting requirements, more clearly emphasize those terms that can significantly affect cardholder costs, such as the actions that can cause default or other penalty pricing rates to be imposed. We provided a draft of this report to the Federal Reserve, the Office of the Comptroller of the Currency (OCC), the Federal Deposit Insurance Corporation (FDIC), the Federal Trade Commission, the National Credit Union Administration, and the Office of Thrift Supervision for comment. In its written comments, the Federal Reserve agreed that current credit card pricing structures have added to the complexity of card disclosures and indicated that it is studying alternatives for improving both the content and format of disclosures, including involving consumer testing and design consultants.

Background

Credit card use has grown dramatically since the introduction of cards more than 5 decades ago. Cards were first introduced in 1950, when Diners Club established the first general-purpose charge card that allowed its cardholders to purchase goods and services from many different merchants. In the late 1950s, Bank of America began offering the first widely available general purpose credit card, which, unlike a charge card that requires the balance to be paid in full each month, allows a cardholder to make purchases up to a credit limit and pay the balance off over time. To increase the number of consumers carrying the card and to reach retailers outside of Bank of America's area of operation, other banks were given the opportunity to license Bank of America's credit card. As the network of banks issuing these credit cards expanded internationally, administrative operations were spun off into a separate entity that evolved into the Visa network. In contrast to credit cards, debit cards result in funds being withdrawn almost immediately from consumers' bank accounts (as if they had a written a check instead). According to CardWeb.com, Inc., a firm that collects and analyzes data relating to the credit card industry, the number of times per month that credit or debit cards were used for purchases or other transactions exceeded 2.3 billion in May 2003, the last month for which the firm reported this data.

The number of credit cards in circulation and the extent to which they are used has also grown dramatically. The range of goods and services that can be purchased with credit cards has expanded, with cards now being used to pay for groceries, health care, and federal and state income taxes. As shown in figure 1, in 2005, consumers held more than 691 million credit cards and the total value of transactions for which these cards were used exceeded $1.8 trillion.

Figure 1: Credit Cards in Use and Charge Volume, 1980-2005

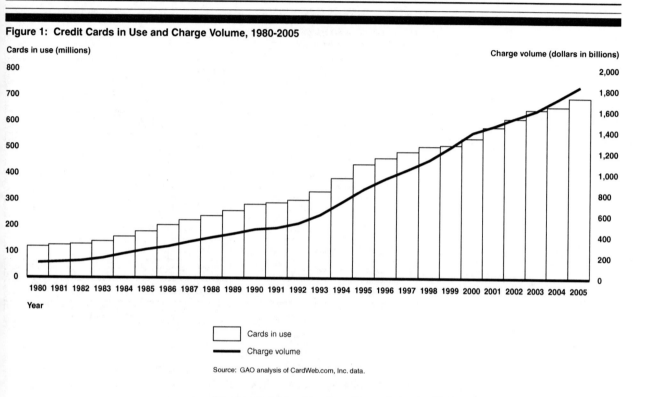

Source: GAO analysis of CardWeb.com, Inc. data.

The largest issuers of credit cards in the United States are commercial banks, including many of the largest banks in the country. More than 6,000 depository institutions issue credit cards, but, over the past decade, the majority of accounts have become increasingly concentrated among a small number of large issuers. Figure 2 shows the largest bank issuers of credit cards by their total credit card balances outstanding as of December 31, 2004 (the most recent data available) and the proportion they represent of the overall total of card balances outstanding.

Figure 2: The 10 Largest Credit Card Issuers by Credit Card Balances Outstanding as of December 31, 2004

Card issuer	Outstanding receivables	Percent of total market	
Citigroup Inc.	$139,600,000,000		20.2
Chase Card Services	135,370,000,000		19.5
MBNA America	101,900,000,000		14.7
Bank of America	58,629,000,000		8.5
Capital One Financial Corp.	48,609,571,000		7.0
Discover Financial Services, Inc.	48,261,000,000		7.0
American Express Centurion Bank	39,600,000,000		5.7
HSBC Credit Card Services	19,670,000,000		2.8
Providian Financial Corp.	18,100,000,000		2.6
Wells Fargo	13,479,889,059		1.9
	$623,219,460,059		90.0

Source: GAO analysis of Card Industry Directory data.

TILA is the primary federal law pertaining to the extension of consumer credit. Congress passed TILA in 1968 to provide for meaningful disclosure of credit terms in order to enable consumers to more easily compare the various credit terms available in the marketplace, to avoid the uninformed use of credit, and to protect themselves against inaccurate and unfair credit billing and credit card practices. The regulation that implements TILA's requirements is Regulation Z, which is administered by the Federal Reserve.

Under Regulation Z, card issuers are required to disclose the terms and conditions to potential and existing cardholders at various times. When first marketing a card directly to prospective cardholders, written or oral applications or solicitations to open credit card accounts must generally disclose key information relevant to the costs of using the card, including the applicable interest rate that will be assessed on any outstanding balances and several key fees or other charges that may apply, such as the fee for making a late payment.[14] In addition, issuers must provide consumers with an initial disclosure statement, which is usually a component of the issuer's cardmember agreement, before the first transaction is made with a card. The cardmember agreement provides more comprehensive information about a card's terms and conditions than would be provided as part of the application or a solicitation letter.

In some cases, the laws of individual states also can affect card issuers' operations. For example, although many credit card agreements permit issuers to make unilateral changes to the agreement's terms and conditions, some state laws require that consumers be given the right to opt out of changes. However, as a result of the National Bank Act, and its interpretation by the U.S. Supreme Court, the interest and fees charged by a national bank on credit card accounts is subject only to the laws of the state in which the bank is chartered, even if its lending activities occur outside of its charter state.[15] As a result, the largest banks have located their credit card operations in states with laws seen as more favorable for the issuer with respect to credit card lending.

Various federal agencies oversee credit card issuers. The Federal Reserve has responsibility for overseeing issuers that are chartered as state banks and are also members of the Federal Reserve System. Many card issuers are chartered as national banks, which OCC supervises. Other regulators of bank issuers are FDIC, which oversees state-chartered banks with federally insured deposits that are not members of the Federal Reserve System; the Office of Thrift Supervision, which oversees federally chartered and state-chartered savings associations with federally insured deposits; or the

---

[14]Issuers have several disclosure options with respect to applications or solicitations made available to the general public, including those contained in catalogs or magazines. Specifically, on such applications or solicitations issuers may, but are not required to, disclose the same key pricing terms required to be disclosed on direct mail applications and solicitations. Alternatively, issuers may include in a prominent location on the application or solicitation a statement that costs are associated with use of the card and a toll-free telephone number and mailing address where the consumer may contact the issuer to request specific information. 12 C.F.R. § 226.5a(e)(3).

[15]The National Bank Act provision codified at 12 U.S.C. § 85 permits national banks to charge interest at a rate allowed by laws of the jurisdiction in which the bank is located. In *Marquette National Bank v. First of Omaha Service Corp. et al.*, 439 U.S. 299 (1978), the U.S. Supreme Court held that a national bank is deemed to be "located" in the state in which it is chartered. *See also Smiley v. Citibank (South Dakota)*, N.A., 517 U.S. 735 (1996) (holding that "interest" under 12 U.S.C. § 85 includes any charges attendant to credit card usage).

National Credit Union Administration, which oversees federally-chartered and state-chartered credit unions whose member accounts are federally insured. As part of their oversight, these regulators review card issuers' compliance with TILA and ensure that an institution's credit card operations do not pose a threat to the institutions' safety and soundness. The Federal Trade Commission generally has responsibility for enforcing TILA and other consumer protection laws for credit card issuers that are not depository institutions.

Credit Card Fees and Issuer Practices That Can Increase Cardholder Costs Have Expanded, but a Minority of Cardholders Appear to Be Affected

Prior to about 1990, card issuers offered credit cards that featured an annual fee, a relatively high, fixed interest rate, and low penalty fees, compared with average rates and fees assessed in 2005. Over the past 15 years, typical credit cards offered by the largest U.S. issuers evolved to feature more complex pricing structures, including multiple interest rates that vary with market fluctuations. The largest issuers also increased the number, and in some cases substantially increased the amounts, of fees assessed on cardholders for violations of the terms of their credit agreement, such as making a late payment. Issuers said that these changes have benefited a greater number of cardholders, whereas critics contended that some practices unfairly increased cardholder costs. The largest six issuers provided data indicating that most of their cardholders had interest rates on their cards that were lower than the single fixed rates that prevailed on cards prior to the 1990s and that a small proportion of cardholders paid high penalty interest rates in 2005. In addition, although most cardholders did not appear to be paying penalty fees, about one-third of the accounts with these largest issuers paid at least one late fee in 2005.

Issuers Have Developed More Complex Credit Card Pricing Structures

The interest rates, fees, and other practices that represent the pricing structure for credit cards have become more complex since the early 1990s. After first being introduced in the 1950s, for the next several decades, credit cards commonly charged a single fixed interest rate around 20 percent—as the annual percentage rate (APR)—which covered most of an issuer's expenses associated with card use.[16] Issuers also charged cardholders an annual fee, which was typically between $20 and $50

---

[16]Unless otherwise noted, in this report we will use the term "interest rate" to describe annual percentage rates, which represent the rates expressed on an annual basis even though interest may be assessed more frequently.

beginning in about 1980, according to a senior economist at the Federal Reserve Board. Card issuers generally offered these credit cards only to the most creditworthy U.S. consumers. According to a study of credit card pricing done by a member of the staff of one of the Federal Reserve Banks, few issuers in the late 1980s and early 1990s charged cardholders fees as penalties if they made late payments or exceeded the credit limit set by the issuer.[17] Furthermore, these fees, when they were assessed, were relatively small. For example, the Federal Reserve Bank staff member's paper notes that the typical late fee charged on cards in the 1980s ranged from $5 to $10.

Multiple Interest Rates May Apply to a Single Account and May Change Based on Market Fluctuations

After generally charging just a single fixed interest rate before 1990, the largest issuers now apply multiple interest rates to a single card account balance and the level of these rates can vary depending on the type of transaction in which a cardholder engages. To identify recent pricing trends for credit cards, we analyzed the disclosures made to prospective and existing cardholders for 28 popular credit cards offered during 2003, 2004, and 2005 by the six largest issuers (based on credit card balances outstanding at the end of 2004).[18] At that time, these issuers held almost 80 percent of consumer debt owed to credit card issuers and as much as 61 percent of total U.S. credit card accounts. As a result, our analysis of these 28 cards likely describes the card pricing structure and terms that apply to the majority of U.S. cardholders. However, our sample of cards did not include subprime cards, which typically have higher cost structures to compensate for the higher risks posed by subprime borrowers.

We found that all but one of these popular cards assessed up to three different interest rates on a cardholder's balance. For example, cards assessed separate rates on

- balances that resulted from the purchase or lease of goods and services, such as food, clothing, and home appliances;

---

[17]M. Furletti, "Credit Card Pricing Developments and Their Disclosure," Federal Reserve Bank of Philadelphia's Payment Cards Center, January 2003. In preparing this paper, the author relied on public data, proprietary issuer data, and data from a review of more than 150 cardmember agreements from 15 of the largest issuers in the United States for the 5-year period spanning 1997 to 2002.

[18]See *Card Industry Directory: The Blue Book of the Credit and Debit Card Industry in North America*, 17th Edition, (Chicago, IL: 2005). These issuers were Bank of America, Capital One Bank; Chase Bank USA: Citibank (South Dakota), N.A.; Discover Financial Services; and MBNA America Bank.

- balances that were transferred from another credit card, which cardholders may do to consolidate balances across cards to take advantage of lower interest rates; and

- balances that resulted from using the card to obtain cash, such as a withdrawal from a bank automated teller machine.

In addition to having separate rates for different transactions, popular credit cards increasingly have interest rates that vary periodically as market interest rates change. Almost all of the cards we analyzed charged variable rates, with the number of cards assessing these rates having increased over the most recent 3-year period. More specifically, about 84 percent of cards we reviewed (16 of 19 cards) assessed a variable interest rate in 2003, 91 percent (21 of 23 cards) in 2004, and 93 percent (25 of 27 cards) in 2005.[19] Issuers typically determine these variable rates by taking the prevailing level of a base rate, such as the prime rate, and adding a fixed percentage amount.[20] In addition, the issuers usually reset the interest rates on a monthly basis.

Issuers appear to have assessed lower interest rates in recent years than they did prior to about 1990. Issuer representatives noted that issuers used to generally offer cards with a single rate of around 20 percent to their cardholders, and the average credit card rates reported by the Federal Reserve were generally around 18 percent between 1972 and 1990. According to the survey of credit card plans, conducted every 6 months by the Federal Reserve, more than 100 card issuers indicated that these issuers charged interest rates between 12 and 15 percent on average from 2001 to 2005. For the 28 popular cards we reviewed, the average interest rate that would be assessed for purchases was 12.3 percent in 2005, almost 6 percentage points lower than the average rates that prevailed until about 1990. We found that the range of rates charged on these cards was between about 8 and 19 percent in 2005. The average rate on these cards climbed slightly during this period, having averaged about 11.5 percent in 2003 and about 12 percent in 2004, largely reflecting the general upward movement

---

[19]Although we reviewed a total of 28 card products for 2003 to 2005, we did not obtain disclosure documents for all card products for every year.

[20]The prime rate is the rate that commercial banks charge to the most creditworthy borrowers, such as large corporations for short-term loans. The prime rate reported by *The Wall Street Journal* is often used as a benchmark for credit card loans made in the United States.

in prime rates. Figure 3 shows the general decline in credit card interest rates, as reported by the Federal Reserve, between about 1991 and 2005 compared with the prime rate over this time. As these data show, credit card interest rates generally were stable regardless of the level of market interest rates until around 1996, at which time changes in credit card rates approximated changes in market interest rates. In addition, the spread between the prime rate and credit card rates was generally wider in the period before the 1980s than it has been since 1990, which indicates that since then cardholders are paying lower rates in terms of other market rates.

Figure 3: Credit Card Interest Rates, 1972-2005

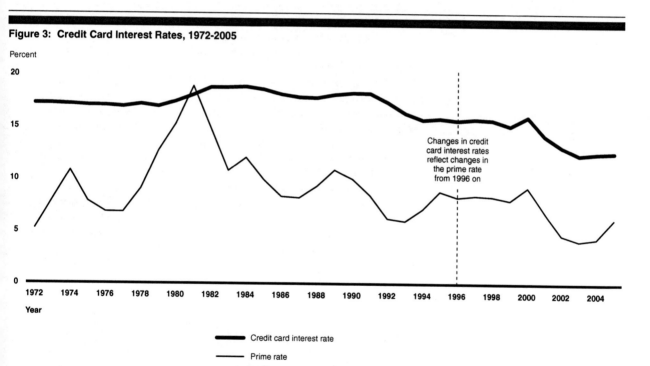

Source: GAO analysis of Federal Reserve data.

Recently, many issuers have attempted to obtain new customers by offering low, even zero, introductory interest rates for limited periods. According to an issuer representative and industry analyst we interviewed, low introductory interest rates have been necessary to attract cardholders in the current competitive environment where most consumers who qualify for a credit card already have at least one. Of the 28 popular cards that we analyzed, 7 cards (37 percent) offered prospective cardholders a low introductory rate in 2003, but 20 (74 percent) did so in 2005—with most rates set at zero for about 8 months. According to an analyst who studies the credit card industry for large investors, approximately 25 percent of all purchases are made with cards offering a zero percent interest rate.

Increased competition among issuers, which can be attributed to several factors, likely caused the reductions in credit card interest rates. In the early 1990s, new banks whose operations were solely focused on credit cards entered the market, according to issuer representatives. Known as monoline banks, issuer representatives told us these institutions competed for cardholders by offering lower interest rates and rewards, and expanded the availability of credit to a much larger segment of the population. Also, in 1988, new requirements were implemented for credit card disclosures that were intended to help consumers better compare pricing information on credit cards. These new requirements mandated that card issuers use a tabular format to provide information to consumers about interest rates and some fees on solicitations and applications mailed to consumers. According to issuers, consumer groups, and others, this format, which is popularly known as the Schumer box, has helped to significantly increase consumer awareness of credit card costs.[21] According to a study authored by a staff member of a Federal Reserve Bank, consumer awareness of credit card interest rates has prompted more cardholders to transfer card balances from one issuer to another, further increasing competition among issuers.[22] However, another study prepared by the Federal Reserve Board also attributes declines in credit card interest rates to a sharp drop in issuers' cost of funds, which is the price issuers pay other lenders to obtain the funds that are then lent to cardholders.[23] (We discuss issuers' cost of funds later in this report.)

---

[21]The Schumer box is the result of the Fair Credit and Charge Card Disclosure Act, Pub. L. No. 100-583, 102 Stat. 2960 (1988), which amended TILA to provide for more detailed and uniform disclosures of rates and other cost information in applications and solicitations to open credit and charge card accounts. The act also required issuers to disclose pricing information, to the extent practicable as determined by the Federal Reserve, in a tabular format. This table is also known as the Schumer box, named for the Congressman that introduced the provision requiring this disclosure into the legislation.

[22]Furletti, "Credit Card Pricing Developments and Their Disclosure."

[23]Board of Governors of the Federal Reserve System, *The Profitability of Credit Card Operations of Depository Institutions*, (Washington, D.C.: June 2005).

Our analysis of disclosures also found that the rates applicable to balance transfers were generally the same as those assessed for purchases, but the rates for cash advances were often higher. Of the popular cards offered by the largest issuers, nearly all featured rates for balance transfers that were substantially similar to their purchase rates, with many also offering low introductory rates on balance transfers for about 8 months. However, the rates these cards assessed for obtaining a cash advance were around 20 percent on average. Similarly to rates for purchases, the rates for cash advances on most cards were also variable rates that would change periodically with market interest rates.

Credit Cards Increasingly Have Assessed Higher Penalty Fees

Although featuring lower interest rates than in earlier decades, typical cards today now include higher and more complex fees than they did in the past for making late payments, exceeding credit limits, and processing returned payments. One penalty fee, commonly included as part of credit card terms, is the late fee, which issuers assess when they do not receive at least the minimum required payment by the due date indicated in a cardholder's monthly billing statement. As noted earlier, prior to 1990, the level of late fees on cards generally ranged from $5 to $10. However, late fees have risen significantly. According to data reported by CardWeb.com, Inc., credit card late fees rose from an average of $12.83 in 1995 to $33.64 in 2005, an increase of over 160 percent. Adjusted for inflation, these fees increased about 115 percent on average, from $15.61 in 1995 to $33.64 in 2005.[24] Similarly, Consumer Action, a consumer interest group that conducts an annual survey of credit card costs, found late fees rose from an average of $12.53 in 1995 to $27.46 in 2005, a 119 percent increase (or 80 percent after adjusting for inflation).[25] Figure 4 shows trends in average late fee assessments reported by these two groups.

---

[24]Dollar values adjusted using the Gross Domestic Product (GDP) deflator, with 2005 as the base year.

[25]Consumer Action analyzed more than 100 card products offered by more than 40 issuers in each year they conducted the survey, except in 1995, when 71 card products were included.

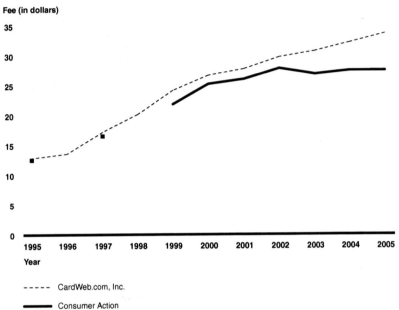

Figure 4: Average Annual Late Fees Reported from Issuer Surveys, 1995-2005 (unadjusted for inflation)

Fee (in dollars)

Year

- - - - - CardWeb.com, Inc.

———— Consumer Action

Source: GAO analysis of Consumer Action Credit Card Survey, CardWeb.com, Inc.

Notes: Consumer Action data did not report values for 1996 and 1998.

CardWeb.com, Inc. data are for financial institutions with more than $100 million in outstanding receivables.

In addition to increased fees a cardholder may be charged per occurrence, many cards created tiered pricing that depends on the balance held by the cardholder.[26] Between 2003 and 2005, all but 4 of the 28 popular cards that we analyzed used a tiered fee structure. Generally, these cards included three tiers, with the following range of fees for each tier:

- $15 to $19 on accounts with balances of $100 or $250;

- $25 to $29 on accounts with balances up to about $1,000; and

---

[26]Based on our analysis of the Consumer Action survey data, issuers likely began introducing tiered late fees in 2002.

GAO-06-929 Credit Cards

- $34 to $39 on accounts with balances of about $1,000 or more.

Tiered pricing can prevent issuers from assessing high fees to cardholders with comparatively small balances. However, data from the Federal Reserve's Survey of Consumer Finances, which is conducted every 3 years, show that the median total household outstanding balance on U.S. credit cards was about $2,200 in 2004 among those that carried balances. When we calculated the late fees that would be assessed on holders of the 28 cards if they had the entire median balance on one card, the average late fee increased from $34 in 2003 to $37 in 2005, with 18 of the cards assessing the highest fee of $39 in 2005.

Issuers also assess cardholders a penalty fee for exceeding the credit limit set by the issuer. In general, issuers assess over-limit fees when a cardholder exceeds the credit limit set by the card issuer. Similar to late fees, over-limit fees also have been rising and increasingly involve a tiered structure. According to data reported by CardWeb.com, Inc., the average over-limit fees that issuers assessed increased 138 percent from $12.95 in 1995 to $30.81 in 2005. Adjusted for inflation, average over-limit fees reported by CardWeb.com increased from $15.77 in 1995 to $30.81 in 2005, representing about a 95 percent increase.[27] Similarly, Consumer Action found a 114 percent increase in this period (or 76 percent, after adjusting for inflation). Figure 5 illustrates the trend in average over-limit fees over the past 10 years from these two surveys.

---

[27]Dollar values adjusted using the Gross Domestic Product (GDP) deflator, with 2005 as the base year.

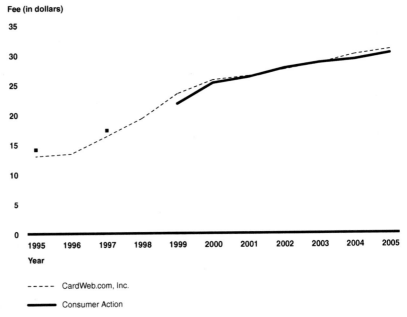

Figure 5: Average Annual Over-limit fees Reported from Issuer Surveys, 1995-2005 (unadjusted for inflation)

Fee (in dollars)

CardWeb.com, Inc.

Consumer Action

Source: GAO analysis of Consumer Action Credit Card Survey, CardWeb.com, Inc.

Notes: Consumer Action did not report values for 1996 and 1998.

CardWeb.com, Inc. data are for financial institutions with more than $100 million in outstanding receivables.

The cards we analyzed also increasingly featured tiered structures for over-limit fees, with 29 percent (5 of 17 cards) having such structures in 2003, and 53 percent (10 of 19 cards) in 2005. Most cards that featured tiered over-limit fees assessed the highest fee on accounts with balances greater than $1,000. But not all over-limit tiers were based on the amount of the cardholder's outstanding balance. Some cards based the amount of the over-limit fee on other indicators, such as the amount of the cardholder's credit limit or card type. For the six largest issuers' popular cards with over-limit fees, the average fee that would be assessed on accounts that carried the median U.S. household credit card balance of $2,200 rose from $32 in 2003 to $34 in 2005. Among cards that assessed over-limit fees in 2005, most charged an amount between $35 and $39.

Not all of the 28 popular large-issuer cards included over-limit fees and the prevalence of such fees may be declining. In 2003, 85 percent, or 17 of 20 cards, had such fees, but only 73 percent, or 19 of 26 cards, did in 2005. According to issuer representatives, they are increasingly emphasizing competitive strategies that seek to increase the amount of spending that their existing cardholders do on their cards as a way to generate revenue. This could explain a movement away from assessing over-limit fees, which likely discourage cardholders who are near their credit limit from spending.

Cards also varied in when an over-limit fee would be assessed. For example, our analysis of the 28 popular large-issuer cards showed that, of the 22 cards that assessed over-limit fees, about two-thirds (14 of 22) would assess an over-limit fee if the cardholder's balance exceeded the credit limit within a billing cycle, whereas the other cards (8 of 22) would assess the fee only if a cardholder's balance exceeded the limit at the end of the billing cycle. In addition, within the overall limit, some of the cards had separate credit limits on the card for how much a cardholder could obtain in cash or transfer from other cards or creditors, before similarly triggering an over-limit fee.

Finally, issuers typically assess fees on cardholders for submitting a payment that is not honored by the issuer or the cardholder's paying bank. Returned payments can occur when cardholders submit a personal check that is written for an amount greater than the amount in their checking account or submit payments that cannot be processed. In our analysis of 28 popular cards offered by the six largest issuers, we found the average fee charged for such returned payments remained steady between 2003 and 2005 at about $30.

Cards Now Frequently Include a Range of Other Fees

Since 1990, issuers have appended more fees to credit cards. In addition to penalties for the cardholder actions discussed above, the 28 popular cards now often include fees for other types of transactions or for providing various services to cardholders. As shown in table 1, issuers assess fees for such services as providing cash advances or for making a payment by telephone. According to our analysis, not all of these fees were disclosed in the materials that issuers generally provide to prospective or existing cardholders. Instead, card issuers told us that they notified their customers of these fees by other means, such as telephone conversations.

Table 1: Various Fees for Services and Transactions, Charged in 2005 on Popular Large-Issuer Cards

Fee type	Assessed for:	Number of cards that assessed fee in 2005	Average or range of amounts generally assessed (if charged)
Cash advance	Obtaining cash or cash equivalent item using credit card or convenience checks	26 of 27	3% of cash advance amount or $5 minimum
Balance transfer	Transferring all or part of a balance from another creditor	15 of 27	3% of transfer amount or $5 to $10 minimum
Foreign transaction	Making purchases in a foreign country or currency	19 of 27	3% of transaction amount (in U.S. dollars)
Returned convenience check	Using a convenience check that the issuer declines to honor	20 of 27	$31
Stop payment	Requesting to stop payment on a convenience check written against the account	20 of 27	$26
Telephone payment	Arranging a single payment through a customer service agent	N/A[a]	$5-$15
Duplicate copy of account records	Obtaining a copy of a billing statement or other record	N/A[a]	$2-$13 per item
Rush delivery of credit card	Requesting that a card be sent by overnight delivery	N/A[a]	$10-$20

Source: GAO.

Note: Cash equivalent transactions include the purchase of items such as money orders, lottery tickets and casino chips. Convenience checks are personalized blank checks that issuers provide cardholders that can be written against the available credit limit of a credit card account.

[a]We were unable to determine the number of cards that assessed telephone payment, duplicate copy, or rush delivery fees in 2005 because these fees are not required by regulation to be disclosed with either mailed solicitation letters or initial disclosure statements. We obtained information about the level of these fees from a survey of the six largest U.S. issuers.

While issuers generally have been including more kinds of fees on credit cards, one category has decreased: most cards offered by the largest issuers do not require cardholders to pay an annual fee. An annual fee is a fixed fee that issuers charge cardholders each year they continue to own that card. Almost 75 percent of cards we reviewed charged no annual fee in 2005 (among those that did, the range was from $30 to $90). Also, an industry group representative told us that approximately 2 percent of cards featured annual fee requirements. Some types of cards we reviewed were more likely to apply an annual fee than others. For example, cards that offered airline tickets in exchange for points that accrue to a cardholder for using the card were likely to apply an annual fee. However, among the 28 popular cards that we reviewed, not all of the cards that offered rewards charged annual fees.

Recently, some issuers have introduced cards without certain penalty fees. For example, one of the top six issuers has introduced a card that does not charge a late fee, over-limit fee, cash-advance fee, returned payment fee, or an annual fee. Another top-six issuer's card does not charge the cardholder a late fee as long as one purchase is made during the billing cycle. However, the issuer of this card may impose higher interest rates, including above 30 percent, if the cardholder pays late or otherwise defaults on the terms of the card.

Issuers Have Introduced Various Practices that Can Significantly Affect Cardholder Costs

Popular credit cards offered by the six largest issuers involve various issuer practices that can significantly affect the costs of using a credit card for a cardholder. These included practices such as raising a card's interest rates in response to cardholder behaviors and how payments are allocated across balances.

Interest Rate Changes

One of the practices that can significantly increase the costs of using typical credit cards is penalty pricing. Under this practice, the interest rate applied to the balances on a card automatically can be increased in response to behavior of the cardholder that appears to indicate that the cardholder presents greater risk of loss to the issuer. For example, representatives for one large issuer told us they automatically increase a cardholder's interest rate if a cardholder makes a late payment or exceeds the credit limit. Card disclosure documents now typically include information about default rates, which represent the maximum penalty rate that issuers can assess in response to cardholders' violations of the terms of the card. According to an industry specialist at the Federal Reserve, issuers first began the practice of assessing default interest rates as a penalty for term violations in the late 1990s. As of 2005, all but one of the cards we reviewed included default rates. The default rates were generally much higher than rates that otherwise applied to purchases, cash advances, or balance transfers. For example, the average default rate across the 28 cards was 27.3 percent in 2005—up from the average of 23.8 percent in 2003—with as many as 7 cards charging rates over 30 percent. Like many of the other rates assessed on these cards in 2005, default rates generally were variable rates. Increases in average default rates between 2003 and 2005 resulted from increases both in the prime rate, which rose about 2 percentage points during this time, and the average fixed amount that issuers added. On average, the fixed amount that issuers added to the index rate in setting default rate levels increased from about 19 percent in 2003 to 22 percent in 2005.

Four of the six largest issuers typically included conditions in their disclosure documents that could allow the cardholder's interest rate to be reduced from a higher penalty rate. For example some issuers would lower a cardholders' rate for not paying late and otherwise abiding by the terms of the card for a period of 6 or 12 consecutive months after the default rate was imposed. However, at least one issuer indicated that higher penalty rates would be charged on existing balances even after six months of good behavior. This issuer assessed lower nonpenalty rates only on new purchases or other new balances, while continuing to assess higher penalty rates on the balance that existed when the cardholder was initially assessed a higher penalty rate. This practice may significantly increase costs to cardholders even after they've met the terms of their card agreement for at least six months.

The specific conditions under which the largest issuers could raise a cardholder's rate to the default level on the popular cards that we analyzed varied. The disclosures for 26 of the 27 cards that included default rates in 2005 stated that default rates could be assessed if the cardholders made late payments. However, some cards would apply such default rates only after multiple violations of card terms. For example, issuers of 9 of the cards automatically would increase a cardholder's rates in response to two late payments. Additionally, for 18 of the 28 cards, default rates could apply for exceeding the credit limit on the card, and 10 cards could also impose such rates for returned payments. Disclosure documents for 26 of the 27 cards that included default rates also indicated that in response to these violations of terms, the interest rate applicable to purchases could be increased to the default rate. In addition, such violations would also cause issuers to increase the rates applicable to cash advances on 16 of the cards, as well as increase rates applicable to balance transfers on 24 of the cards.

According to a paper by a Federal Reserve Bank researcher, some issuers began to increase cardholders' interest rates in the early 2000s for actions they took with other creditors.[28] According to this paper, these issuers would increase rates when cardholders failed to make timely payments to other creditors, such as other credit card issuers, utility companies, and mortgage lenders. Becoming generally known as "universal default," consumer groups criticized these practices. In 2004, OCC issued guidance to the banks that it oversees, which include many of the largest card

---

[28]Furletti, "Credit Card Pricing Developments and Their Disclosure."

issuers, which addressed such practices.[29] While OCC noted that the repricing might be an appropriate way for banks to manage their credit risk, they also noted that such practices could heighten a bank's compliance and reputation risks. As a result, OCC urged national banks to fully and prominently disclose in promotional materials the circumstances under which a cardholder's interest rates, fees, or other terms could be changed and whether the bank reserved the right to change these unilaterally. Around the time of this guidance, issuers generally ceased automatically repricing cardholders to default interest rates for risky behavior exhibited with other creditors. Of the 28 popular large issuer cards that we reviewed, three cards in 2005 included terms that would allow the issuer to automatically raise a cardholder's rate to the default rate if they made a late payment to another creditor.

Although the six largest U.S. issuers appear to have generally ceased making automatic increases to a default rate for behavior with other creditors, some continue to employ practices that allow them to seek to raise a cardholder's interest rates in response to behaviors with other creditors. During our review, representatives of four of these issuers told us that they may seek to impose higher rates on a cardholder in response to behaviors related to other creditors but that such increases would be done as a change-in-terms, which can require prior notification, rather than automatically.[30] Regulation Z requires that the affected cardholders be notified in writing of any such proposed changes in rate terms at least 15 days before such change becomes effective.[31] In addition, under the laws of the states in which four of the six largest issuers are chartered, cardholders would have to be given the right to opt out of the change.[32] However, issuer representatives told us that few cardholders exercise this right. The ability of cardholders to opt out of such increases also has been questioned. For example, one legal essay noted that some cardholders may not be able to reject the changed terms of their cards if the result would be a requirement

---

[29]Credit Card Practices, OCC Advisory Letter AL 2004-10 (Sept. 14, 2004).

[30]At least one of the six largest issuers may automatically increase a cardholder's rates for violations of terms on any loan the cardholder held with the issuer or bank with which it was affiliated.

[31]12 C.F.R. § 226.9(c).

[32]States in which issuers have a statutory obligation to afford cardholders an opportunity to opt-out or reject a change-in-terms to increase the interest rate on their credit card account include Delaware, South Dakota, New Hampshire, Florida and Georgia.

to pay off the balance immediately.[33] In addition, an association for community banks that provided comments to the Federal Reserve as part of the ongoing review of card disclosures noted that 15 days does not provide consumers sufficient time to make other credit arrangements if the new terms were undesirable.

Payment Allocation Method

The way that issuers allocate payments across balances also can increase the costs of using the popular cards we reviewed. In this new credit environment where different balances on a single account may be assessed different interest rates, issuers have developed practices for allocating the payments cardholders make to pay down their balance. For 23 of the 28 popular larger-issuer cards that we reviewed, cardholder payments would be allocated first to the balance that is assessed the lowest rate of interest.[34] As a result, the low interest balance would have to be fully paid before any of the cardholder's payment would pay down balances assessed higher rates of interest. This practice can prolong the length of time that issuers collect finance charges on the balances assessed higher rates of interest.

Balance Computation Method

Additionally, some of the cards we reviewed use a balance computation method that can increase cardholder costs. On some cards, issuers have used a double-cycle billing method, which eliminates the interest-free period of a consumer who moves from nonrevolving to revolving status, according to Federal Reserve staff. In other words, in cases where a cardholder, with no previous balance, fails to pay the entire balance of new purchases by the payment due date, issuers compute interest on the original balance that previously had been subject to an interest-free period. This method is illustrated in figure 6.

---

[33]Samuel Issacharoff and Erin F. Delaney, "Symposium: Homo Economicus, Homo Myopicus, and the Law and Economics of Consumer Choice," *University of Chicago Law Review* 73 (Winter: 2006).

[34]Issuers of the remaining five cards would apply cardholder payments in a manner subject to their discretion.

Figure 6: How the Double-Cycle Billing Method Works

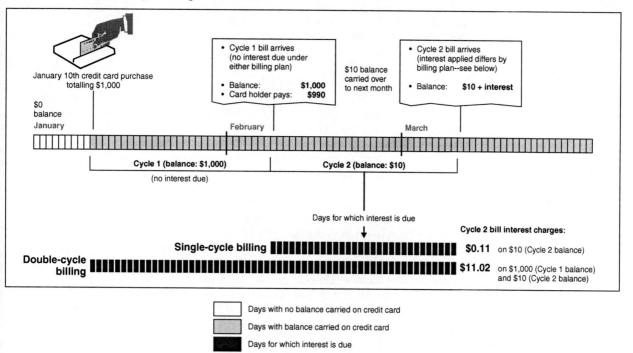

Days with no balance carried on credit card

Days with balance carried on credit card

Days for which interest is due

Sources: GAO analysis of Federal Reserve Bank data; Art Explosion (images).

Note: We calculated finance charges assuming a 13.2 percent APR, 30-day billing cycle, and that the cardholder's payment is credited on the first day of cycle 2. We based our calculations on an average daily balance method and daily compounding of finance charges.

In our review of 28 popular cards from the six largest issuers, we found that two of the six issuers used the double-cycle billing method on one or more popular cards between 2003 and 2005. The other four issuers indicated they would only go back one cycle to impose finance charges.

New Practices Appear to Affect a Minority of Cardholders

Representatives of issuers, consumer groups, and others we interviewed generally disagreed over whether the evolution of credit card pricing and other practices has been beneficial to consumers. However, data provided by the six largest issuers show that many of their active accounts did not pay finance charges and that a minority of their cardholders were affected by penalty charges in 2005.

Issuers Say Practices Benefit More Cardholders, but Critics Say Some Practices Harm Consumers

The movement towards risk-based pricing for cards has allowed issuers to offer better terms to some cardholders and more credit cards to others. Spurred by increased competition, many issuers have adopted risk-based pricing structures in which they assess different rates on cards depending on the credit quality of the borrower. Under this pricing structure, issuers have offered cards with lower rates to more creditworthy borrowers, but also have offered credit to consumers who previously would not have been considered sufficiently creditworthy. For example, about 70 percent of families held a credit card in 1989, but almost 75 percent held a card by 2004, according to the Federal Reserve Board's Survey of Consumer Finances. Cards for these less creditworthy consumers have featured higher rates to reflect the higher repayment risk that such consumers represented. For example, the initial purchase rates on the 28 popular cards offered by the six largest issuers ranged from about 8 percent to 19 percent in 2005.

According to card issuers, credit cards offer many more benefits to users than they did in the past. For example, according to the six largest issuers, credit cards are an increasingly convenient and secure form of payment. These issuers told us credit cards are accepted at more than 23 million merchants worldwide, can be used to make purchases or obtain cash, and are the predominant form of payment for purchases made on the Internet. They also told us that rewards, such as cash-back and airline travel, as well as other benefits, such as rental car insurance or lost luggage protection, also have become standard. Issuers additionally noted that credit cards are reducing the need for cash. Finally, they noted that cardholders typically are not responsible for loss, theft, fraud, or misuse of their credit cards by unauthorized users, and issuers often assist cardholders that are victims of identity theft.

In contrast, according to some consumer groups and others, the newer pricing structures have resulted in many negative outcomes for some consumers. Some consumer advocates noted adverse consequences of offering credit, especially at higher interest rates, to less creditworthy consumers. For example, lower-income or young consumers, who do not have the financial means to carry credit card debt, could worsen their financial condition.[35] In addition, consumer groups and academics said that

---

[35]We previously reported on the marketing of credit cards to students and student experiences with credit cards. See GAO *Consumer Finance: College Students and Credit Cards*, GAO-01-773, (Washington, D.C.: June 20, 2001).

various penalty fees could increase significantly the costs of using cards for some consumers. Some also argued that card issuers were overly aggressive in their assessment of penalty fees. For instance, a representative of a consumer group noted that issuers do not reject cardholders' purchases during the sale authorization, even if the transaction would put the cardholder over the card's credit limit, and yet will likely later assess that cardholder an over-limit fee and also may penalize them with a higher interest rate. Furthermore, staff for one banking regulator told us that they have received complaints from consumers who were assessed over-limit fees that resulted from the balance on their accounts going over their credit limit because their card issuer assessed them a late fee. At the same time, credit card issuers have incentives not to be overly aggressive with their assessment of penalty charges. For example, Federal Reserve representatives told us that major card issuers with long-term franchise value are concerned that their banks not be perceived as engaging in predatory lending because this could pose a serious risk to their brand reputation. As a result, they explained that issuers may be wary of charging fees that could be considered excessive or imposing interest rates that might be viewed as potentially abusive. In contrast, these officials noted that some issuers, such as those that focus on lending to consumers with lower credit quality, may be less concerned about their firm's reputation and, therefore, more likely to charge higher fees.

Controversy also surrounds whether higher fees and other charges were commensurate with the risks that issuers faced. Consumer groups and others questioned whether the penalty interest rates and fees were justifiable. For example, one consumer group questioned whether submitting a credit card payment one day late made a cardholder so risky that it justified doubling or tripling the interest rate assessed on that account. Also, as the result of concerns over the level of penalty fees being assessed by banks in the United Kingdom, a regulator there has recently announced that penalty fees greater than 12 pounds (about $23) may be challenged as unfair unless they can be justified by exceptional factors.[36] Representatives of several of the issuers with whom we spoke told us that the levels of the penalty fees they assess generally were set by considering various factors. For example, they noted that higher fees help to offset the increased risk of loss posed by cardholders who pay late or engage in other

---

[36]Office of Fair Trading, *Calculating Fair Default Charges in Credit Card Contracts: A Statement of the OFT's Position*, OFT842 (April 2006).

negative behaviors. Additionally, they noted a 2006 study, which compared the assessment of penalty fees that credit card banks charged to bankruptcy rates in the states in which their cards were marketed, and found that late fee assessments were correlated with bankruptcy rates.[37] Some also noted that increased fee levels reflected increased operating costs; for example, not receiving payments when due can cause the issuer to incur increased costs, such as those incurred by having to call cardholders to request payment. Representatives for four of the largest issuers also told us that their fee levels were influenced by what others in the marketplace were charging.

Concerns also have been expressed about whether consumers adequately consider the potential effect of penalty interest rates and fees when they use their cards. For example, one academic researcher, who has written several papers about the credit card industry, told us that many consumers do not consider the effect of the costs that can accrue to them after they begin using a credit card. According to this researcher, many consumers focus primarily on the amount of the interest rate for purchases when deciding to obtain a new credit card and give less consideration to the level of penalty charges and rates that could apply if they were to miss a payment or violate some other term of their card agreement. An analyst that studies the credit card industry for large investors said that consumers can obtain low introductory rates but can lose them very easily before the introductory period expires.

Most Active Accounts Are Assessed Lower Rates Than in the Past

As noted previously, the average credit card interest rate assessed for purchases has declined from almost 20 percent, that prevailed until the late 1980s, to around 12 percent, as of 2005. In addition, the six largest issuers—whose accounts represent 61 percent of all U.S. accounts—reported to us that the majority of their cardholders in 2005 had cards with interest rates lower than the rate that generally applied to all cardholders prior to about 1990. According to these issuers, about 80 percent of active accounts were assessed interest rates below 20 percent as of December 31, 2005, with

---

[37]Massoud, N., Saunders A., and Scholnick B., "The Cost of Being Late: The Case of Credit Card Penalty Fees," January 2006. Published with financial assistance from the Social Sciences Research Council of Canada and the National Research Program on Financial Services and Public Policy at the Schulich School of Business, York University in Toronto, Ontario (Canada). This study examined data from the Federal Reserve's survey of U.S. credit card rates and fees and compared them to bankruptcy rates across states.

more than 40 percent having rates below 15 percent.[38] However, the proportion of active accounts assessed rates below 15 percent declined since 2003, when 71 percent received such rates. According to issuer representatives, a greater number of active accounts were assessed higher interest rates in 2004 and 2005 primarily because of changes in the prime rate to which many cards' variable rates are indexed. Nevertheless, cardholders today have much greater access to cards with lower interest rates than existed when all cards charged a single fixed rate.

A large number of cardholders appear to avoid paying any significant interest charges. Many cardholders do not revolve a balance from month to month, but instead pay off the balance owed in full at the end of each month. Such cardholders are often referred to as convenience users. According to one estimate, about 42 percent of cardholders are convenience users.[39] As a result, many of these cardholders availed themselves of the benefits of their cards without incurring any direct expenses. Similarly, the six largest issuers reported to us that almost half, or 48 percent, of their active accounts did not pay a finance charge in at least 10 months in 2005, similar to the 47 percent that did so in 2003 and 2004.

Minority of Cardholders Appear to Be Affected by Penalty Charges Assessed by the Largest U.S. Issuers

Penalty interest rates and fees appear to affect a minority of the largest six issuers' cardholders.[40] No comprehensive sources existed to show the extent to which U.S. cardholders were paying penalty interest rates, but, according to data provided by the six largest issuers, a small proportion of their active accounts were being assessed interest rates above 25 percent—which we determined were likely to represent penalty rates. However, this proportion had more than doubled over a two-year period by having increased from 5 percent at the end of 2003 to 10 percent in 2004 and 11 percent in 2005.

---

[38]For purposes of this report, active accounts refer to accounts of the top six issuers that had had a debit or credit posted to them by December 31 in 2003, 2004, and 2005.

[39]CardWeb.com, Inc.

[40]Our data likely undercounted the cards and cardholders that were affected by these charges because our data was comprised of active accounts for the six largest U.S. issuers. Although these issuers have some subprime accounts (accounts held by less-creditworthy borrowers), we did not include issuers in our sample that predominantly market to subprime borrowers.

Although still representing a minority of cardholders, cardholders paying at least one type of penalty fee were a significant proportion of all cardholders. According to the six largest issuers, 35 percent of their active accounts had been assessed at least one late fee in 2005. These issuers reported that their late fee assessments averaged $30.92 per active account. Additionally, these issuers reported that they assessed over-limit fees on 13 percent of active accounts in 2005, with an average over-limit fee of $9.49 per active account.

Weaknesses in Credit Card Disclosures Appear to Hinder Cardholder Understanding of Fees and Other Practices That Can Affect Their Costs

The disclosures that issuers representing the majority of credit card accounts use to provide information about the costs and terms of using credit cards had serious weaknesses that likely reduce their usefulness to consumers. These disclosures are the primary means under federal law for protecting consumers against inaccurate and unfair credit card practices. The disclosures we analyzed had weaknesses, such as presenting information written at a level too difficult for the average consumer to understand, and design features, such as text placement and font sizes, that did not conform to guidance for creating easily readable documents. When attempting to use these disclosures, cardholders were often unable to identify key rates or terms and often failed to understand the information in these documents. Several factors help explain these weaknesses, including outdated regulations and guidance. With the intention of improving the information that consumers receive, the Federal Reserve has initiated a comprehensive review of the regulations that govern credit card disclosures. Various suggestions have been made to improve disclosures, including testing them with consumers. While Federal Reserve staff have begun to involve consumers in their efforts, they are still attempting to determine the best form and content of any revised disclosures. Without clear, understandable information, consumers risk making poor choices about using credit cards, which could unnecessarily result in higher costs to use them.

Mandatory Disclosure of Credit Card Terms and Conditions Is the Primary Means Regulators Use for Ensuring Competitive Credit Card Pricing

Having adequately informed consumers that spur competition among issuers is the primary way that credit card pricing is regulated in the United States. Under federal law, a national bank may charge interest on any loan at a rate permitted by the law of the state in which the bank is located.[41] In 1978, the U.S. Supreme Court ruled that a national bank is "located" in the state in which it is chartered, and, therefore, the amount of the interest rates charged by a national bank are subject only to the laws of the state in which it is chartered, even if its lending activities occur elsewhere.[42] As a result, the largest credit card issuing banks are chartered in states that either lacked interest rate caps or had very high caps from which they would offer credit cards to customers in other states. This ability to "export" their chartered states' interest rates effectively removed any caps applicable to interest rates on the cards from these banks. In 1996, the U.S. Supreme Court determined that fees charged on credit extended by national banks are a form of interest, allowing issuers to also export the level of fees allowable in their state of charter to their customers nationwide, which effectively removed any caps on the level of fees that these banks could charge.[43]

In the absence of federal regulatory limitations on the rates and fees that card issuers can assess, the primary means that U.S. banking regulators have for influencing the level of such charges is by facilitating competition among issuers, which, in turn, is highly dependent on informed consumers. The Truth in Lending Act of 1968 (TILA) mandates certain disclosures aimed at informing consumers about the cost of credit. In approving TILA, Congress intended that the required disclosures would foster price competition among card issuers by enabling consumers to discern differences among cards while shopping for credit. TILA also states that its purpose is to assure that the consumer will be able to compare more readily the various credit terms available to him or her and avoid the uninformed use of credit. As authorized under TILA, the Federal Reserve has promulgated Regulation Z to carry out the purposes of TILA. The Federal Reserve, along with the other federal banking agencies, enforces compliance with Regulation Z with respect to the depository institutions under their respective supervision.

In general, TILA and the accompanying provisions of Regulation Z require credit card issuers to inform potential and existing customers about specific pricing terms at specific times. For example, card issuers are

---

[41]12 U.S.C. § 85.

[42]*Marquette National Bank v First of Omaha Service Corp. et. al*, 439 U.S. 299 (1978).

[43]*Smiley v. Citibank*, 517 U.S. 735 (1996).

required to make various disclosures when soliciting potential customers, as well as on the actual applications for credit. On or with card applications and solicitations, issuers generally are required to present pricing terms, including the interest rates and various fees that apply to a card, as well as information about how finance charges are calculated, among other things. Issuers also are required to provide cardholders with specified disclosures prior to the cardholder's first transaction, periodically in billing statements, upon changes to terms and conditions pertaining to the account, and upon account renewal. For example, in periodic statements, which issuers typically provide monthly to active cardholders, issuers are required to provide detailed information about the transactions on the account during the billing cycle, including purchases and payments, and are to disclose the amount of finance charges that accrued on the cardholder's outstanding balance and detail the type and amount of fees assessed on the account, among other things.

In addition to the required timing and content of disclosures, issuers also must adhere to various formatting requirements. For example, since 1989, certain pricing terms must be disclosed in direct mail, telephone, and other applications and solicitations and presented in a tabular format on mailed applications or solicitations.[44] This table, generally referred to as the Schumer box, must contain information about the interest rates and fees that could be assessed to the cardholder, as well as information about how finance charges are calculated, among other things.[45] According to a Federal Reserve representative, the Schumer box is designed to be easy for consumers to read and use for comparing credit cards. According to a consumer group representative, an effective regulatory disclosure is one that stimulates competition among issuers; the introduction of the Schumer box in the late 1980s preceded the increased price competition in the credit card market in the early 1990s and the movement away from uniform credit card products.

Not all fees that are charged by card issuers must be disclosed in the Schumer box. Regulation Z does not require that issuers disclose fees unrelated to the opening of an account. For example, according to the Official Staff Interpretations of Regulation Z (staff interpretations), nonperiodic fees, such as fees charged for reproducing billing statements

---

[44]See generally 12 C.F.R. § 226.5a.

[45]See supra note 21.

or reissuing a lost or stolen card, are not required to be disclosed. Staff interpretations, which are compiled and published in a supplement to Regulation Z, are a means of guiding issuers on the requirements of Regulation Z.[46] Staff interpretations also explain that various fees are not required in initial disclosure statements, such as a fee to expedite the delivery of a credit card or, under certain circumstances, a fee for arranging a single payment by telephone. However, issuers we surveyed told us they inform cardholders about these other fees at the time the cardholders request the service, rather than in a disclosure document.

Although Congress authorized solely the Federal Reserve to adopt regulations to implement the purposes of TILA, other federal banking regulators, under their authority to ensure the safety and soundness of depository institutions, have undertaken initiatives to improve the credit card disclosures made by the institutions under their supervision. For example, the regulator of national banks, OCC, issued an advisory letter in 2004 alerting banks of its concerns regarding certain credit card marketing and account management practices that may expose a bank to compliance and reputation risks. One such practice involved the marketing of promotional interest rates and conditions under which issuers reprice accounts to higher interest rates.[47] In its advisory letter, OCC recommended that issuers disclose any limits on the applicability of promotional interest rates, such as the duration of the rates and the circumstances that could shorten the promotional rate period or cause rates to increase. Additionally, OCC advised issuers to disclose the circumstances under which they could increase a consumer's interest rate or fees, such as for failure to make timely payments to another creditor.

Credit Card Disclosures Typically Provided to Many Consumers Have Various Weaknesses

The disclosures that credit card issuers typically provide to potential and new cardholders had various weaknesses that reduced their usefulness to consumers. These weaknesses affecting the disclosure materials included the typical grade level required to comprehend them, their poor organization and formatting of information, and their excessive detail and length.

---

[46]Compliance with these official staff interpretations afford issuers protection from liability under Section 130(f) of TILA, which protects issuers from civil liability for any act done or omitted in good faith compliance with any official staff interpretation. 12 C.F.R. Part 226, Supp. I.

[47]Credit Card Practices, OCC Advisory Letter AL 2004-10 (Sept. 14, 2004).

Disclosures Written at Too High a Level	The typical credit card disclosure documents contained content that was written at a level above that likely to be understandable by many consumers. To assess the readability of typical credit card disclosures, we contracted with a private usability consultant to evaluate the two primary disclosure documents for four popular, widely-held cards (one each from four large credit card issuers). The two documents were (1) a direct mail solicitation letter and application, which must include information about the costs and fees associated with the card; and (2) the cardmember agreement that contains the full range of terms and conditions applicable to the card.[48] Through visual inspection, we determined that this set of disclosures appeared representative of the disclosures for the 28 cards we reviewed from the six largest issuers that accounted for the majority of cardholders in the United States. To determine the level of education likely needed for someone to understand these disclosures, the usability consultant used computer software programs that applied three widely used readability formulas to the entire text of the disclosures. These formulas determined the readability of written material based on quantitative measures, such as average number of syllables in words or numbers of words in sentences. For more information about the usability consultant's analyses, see appendix I.

On the basis of the usability consultant's analysis, the disclosure documents provided to many cardholders likely were written at a level too high for the average individual to understand. The consultant found that the disclosures on average were written at a reading level commensurate with about a tenth- to twelfth-grade education. According to the consultant's analysis, understanding the disclosures in the solicitation letters would require an eleventh-grade level of reading comprehension, while understanding the cardmember agreements would require about a twelfth-grade education. A consumer advocacy group that tested the reading level needed to understand credit card disclosures arrived at a similar conclusion. In a comment letter to the Federal Reserve, this consumer group noted it had measured a typical passage from a change-in-terms notice on how issuers calculate finance charges using one of the readability formulas and that this passage required a twelfth-grade reading level.

---

[48]We did not evaluate disclosures that issuers are required to provide at other times—such as in periodic billing statements or change in terms notices.

These disclosure documents were written such that understanding them required a higher reading level than that attained by many U.S. cardholders. For example, a nationwide assessment of the reading level of the U.S. population cited by the usability consultant indicated that nearly half of the adult population in the United States reads at or below the eighth-grade level.[49] Similarly, to ensure that the information that public companies are required to disclose to prospective investors is adequately understandable, the Securities and Exchange Commission (SEC) recommends that such disclosure materials be written at a sixth- to eighth-grade level.[50]

In addition to the average reading level, certain portions of the typical disclosure documents provided by the large issuers required even higher reading levels to be understandable. For example, the information that appeared in cardmember agreements about annual percentage rates, grace periods, balance computation, and payment allocation methods required a minimum of a fifteenth-grade education, which is the equivalent of 3 years of college education. Similarly, text in the documents describing the interest rates applicable to one issuer's card were written at a twenty-seventh-grade level. However, not all text in the disclosures required such high levels. For example, the consultant found that the information about fees that generally appeared in solicitation letters required only a seventh- and eighth-grade reading level to be understandable. Solicitation letters likely required lower reading levels to be understandable because they generally included more information in a tabular format than cardmember agreements.

Poor Organization and Formatting

The disclosure documents the consultant evaluated did not use designs, including effective organizational structures and formatting, that would have made them more useful to consumers. To assess the adequacy of the design of the typical large issuer credit card solicitation letters and cardmember agreements, the consultant evaluated the extent to which these disclosures adhered to generally accepted industry standards for

---

[49] 1992 National Adult Literacy Survey. The 2003 National Assessment of Adult Literacy (renamed from 1992) found that reading comprehension levels did not significantly change between 1992 and 2003 and that there was little change in adults' ability to read and understand sentences and paragraphs.

[50] U.S. Securities and Exchange Commission, *Plain English Handbook: How to Create Clear SEC Disclosure Documents* (Washington, D.C.: 1998). The Securities and Exchange Commission regulates the issuance of securities to the public, including the information that companies provide to their investors.

effective organizational structures and designs intended to make documents easy to read. In the absence of best practices and guidelines specifically for credit card disclosures, the consultant used knowledge of plain language, publications design guidelines, and industry best practices and also compared the credit card disclosure documents to the guidelines in the Securities and Exchange Commission's plain English handbook. The usability consultant used these standards to identify aspects of the design of the typical card disclosure documents that could cause consumers using them to encounter problems.

On the basis of this analysis, the usability consultant concluded that the typical credit card disclosures lacked effective organization. For example, the disclosure documents frequently placed pertinent information toward the end of sentences. Figure 7 illustrates an example taken from the cardmember agreement of one of the large issuers that shows that a consumer would need to read through considerable amounts of text before reaching the important information, in this case the amount of the annual percentage rate (APR) for purchases. Best practices would dictate that important information—the amount of the APR—be presented first, with the less important information—the explanation of how the APR is determined—placed last.

Figure 7: Example of Important Information Not Prominently Presented in Typical Credit Card Disclosure Documents

Usability consultant's comments: Placing pertinent information, in this case the APR for purchases, near the end of sentences requires readers to wade through considerable amounts of text before reaching important information.	**3.3.1.a: Purchases.** The Annual Percentage Rate for Purchases, a variable rate, is the Index plus a Margin of 4.99%. Based on this formula, the APR as of May 4, 2005 is 10.99% (0.03011% corresponding Daily Periodic Rate).

Sources: UserWorks, Inc.; Information International Associates.

In addition, the disclosure documents often failed to group relevant information together. Although one of the disclosure formats mandated by law—the Schumer box—has been praised as having simplified the presentation of complex information, our consultant observed that the amount of information that issuers typically presented in the box compromised the benefits of using a tabular format. Specifically, the typical credit card solicitation letter, which includes a Schumer box, may be causing difficulties for consumers because related information generally is not grouped appropriately, as shown in figure 8.

Figure 8: Example of How Related Information Was Not Being Grouped Together in Typical Credit Card Disclosure Documents

Annual Percentage Rate (APR) for Purchases[3]	0.0% fixed introductory rate until October 1, 2006;[1] thereafter, a variable APR, currently 13.49%.• ——————————— Current rate for purchases
Other APRs[3]	**Non-Check Balance Transfers:** 0.0% fixed introductory APR until October 1, 2006;[1] thereafter, together with all other Balance Transfers, a variable APR, currently 13.49%. **Cash Advances and Convenience Checks:** A variable APR, currently 22.49%. **Penalty APR:** A variable APR, currently up to 30.49%.[3]
Variable Rate Information[2]	All APRs (other than your introductory APRs) may vary. They are determined by adding the following margin to the Prime Rate: 6.99 for Purchases and Non-Check Balance Transfers; 15.99% for Cash Advances and Convenience Checks; and up to 23.99% for Penalty APRs. ——— How the rate is determined
Balance Calculation Method for Purchases	Average Daily Balance (including new purchases)
Annual Fee	None
Grace Period for Purchases	At least 20 days
Minimum Finance Charge for Purchases	$1.50 (unless purchase Average Daily Balance is zero)

†*The terms of your Account, including any APR (or how an APR is Calculated) are subject to change. Any changes will be made in accordance with the Cardholder Agreement.*

[1]*If an introductory rate is applicable to this product and we do not receive at least the Minimum Payment Due during any billing cycle, you exceed your credit limit or you close your account, any introductory rate on Purchases and Balance Transfers will terminate.*

[2]*The Prime Rate used in your APR calculations is determined on the last day of each month by taking the highest prime rate published in the Money Rates section of The Wall Street Journal in effect within the prior three months (the "Index Date(s)"). All Prime Rate changes will take effect on the first day of your Billing Cycle that ends in the calendar month following the Index Date. All variable rate disclosures are based on the Prime Rate of 6.50% in effect on August 10, 2005.* ——— How the prime rate is determined

Usability consultant's comments:
Related information, in this case the APR for purchases, is not grouped together, potentially causing difficulties for readers.

Sources: GAO analysis of data from UserWorks, Inc.; Information International Associates.

As shown in figure 8, information about the APR that would apply to purchases made with the card appeared in three different locations. The first row includes the current prevailing rate of the purchase APR; text that describes how the level of the purchase APR could vary according to an underlying rate, such as the prime rate, is included in the third row; and text describing how the issuer determines the level of this underlying rate is included in the footnotes. According to the consultant, grouping such related information together likely would help readers to more easily understand the material.

In addition, of the four issuers whose materials were analyzed, three provided a single document with all relevant information in a single cardmember agreement, but one issuer provided the information in separate documents. For example, this issuer disclosed specific information about the actual amount of rates and fees in one document and presented information about how such rates were determined in another document. According to the readability consultant, disclosures in multiple documents can be more difficult for the reader to use because they may require more work to find information.

Formatting weaknesses also likely reduced the usefulness of typical credit card disclosure documents. The specific formatting issues were as follows:

- *Font sizes.* According to the usability consultant's analysis, many of the disclosure documents used font sizes that were difficult to read and could hinder consumers' ability to find information. For example, the consultant found extensive use of small and condensed typeface in cardmember agreements and in footnotes in solicitation materials when best practices would suggest using a larger, more legible font size. Figure 9 contains an illustration of how the disclosures used condensed text that makes the font appear smaller than it actually is. Multiple consumers and consumer groups who provided comments to the Federal Reserve noted that credit card disclosures were written in a small print that reduces a consumer's ability to read or understand the document. For example, a consumer who provided comments to the Federal Reserve referred to the text in card disclosures as "mice type." This example also illustrates how notes to the text, which should be less important, were the same size and thus given the same visual emphasis as the text inside the box. Consumers attempting to read such disclosures may have difficulty determining which information is more important.

Figure 9: Example of How Use of Small Font Sizes Reduces Readability in Typical Credit Card Disclosure Documents

Condensed 11 pt. text	Regular 11 pt. text

Usability consultant's comments: Using condensed text makes the font appear smaller than it acutally is.

Transaction fees for cash advances	3% of the amount of the advance, bu

Late Payment fee: $14.00 on balances up to, but not including, $150; $28.00 on bal and over. However, if you already have made one or more late payments in the prior

Over-the-Credit-Limit fee: $29.00

International Transactions: 3% of the U.S. dollar amount of the transaction, wheth

[a] You understand that the terms of your account, including the APRs, are subject to change to higher APRs, fixed APRs may change to variable APRs, or variable AI

Transaction fee for purchases made in a foreign currency	3% of the ar U.S. dollars.

Transaction fee for cash advances: 3% of the
Transaction fee for balance transfers: 3% of t
However, there is no fee with the 0% APR balar
Late fee: $15 on balances up to $100; $29 on bi
Over-the-credit-line fee: $35.

*All your APRs may automatically increase up with us because you fail to make a payment

Sources: UserWorks, Inc.; Information International Associates.

Note: Graphic shown is the actual size it appears in issuer disclosure documents. Graphic is intentionally portioned off to focus attention to headings.

- *Ineffective font placements.* According to the usability consultant, some issuers' efforts to distinguish text using different font types sometimes had the opposite effect. The consultant found that the disclosures from all four issuers emphasized large amounts of text with all capital letters and sometimes boldface. According to the consultant, formatting large blocks of text in capitals makes it harder to read because the shapes of the words disappear, forcing the reader to slow down and study each letter (see figure 10). In a comment letter to the Federal Reserve, an industry group recommended that boldfaced or capitalized text should be used discriminately, because in its experience, excessive use of such font types caused disclosures to lose all effectiveness. SEC's guidelines for producing clear disclosures contain similar suggestions.

Figure 10: Example of How Use of Ineffective Font Types Reduces Readability in Typical Credit Card Disclosure Documents

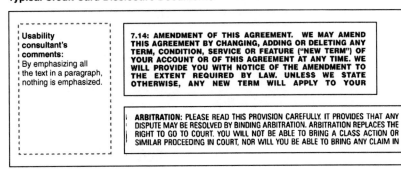

Usability consultant's comments: By emphasizing all the text in a paragraph, nothing is emphasized.

7.14: AMENDMENT OF THIS AGREEMENT. WE MAY AMEND THIS AGREEMENT BY CHANGING, ADDING OR DELETING ANY TERM, CONDITION, SERVICE OR FEATURE ("NEW TERM") OF YOUR ACCOUNT OR OF THIS AGREEMENT AT ANY TIME. WE WILL PROVIDE YOU WITH NOTICE OF THE AMENDMENT TO THE EXTENT REQUIRED BY LAW. UNLESS WE STATE OTHERWISE, ANY NEW TERM WILL APPLY TO YOUR

ARBITRATION: PLEASE READ THIS PROVISION CAREFULLY. IT PROVIDES THAT ANY DISPUTE MAY BE RESOLVED BY BINDING ARBITRATION. ARBITRATION REPLACES THE RIGHT TO GO TO COURT. YOU WILL NOT BE ABLE TO BRING A CLASS ACTION OR SIMILAR PROCEEDING IN COURT, NOR WILL YOU BE ABLE TO BRING ANY CLAIM IN

Sources: UserWorks, Inc.; Information International Associates.

- *Selecting text for emphasis.* According to the usability consultant, most of the disclosure documents unnecessarily emphasized specific terms. Inappropriate emphasis of such material could distract readers from more important messages. Figure 11 contains a passage from one cardmember agreement that the readability consultant singled out for its emphasis of the term "periodic finance charge," which is repeated six times in this example. According to the consultant, the use of boldface and capitalized text calls attention to the word, potentially requiring readers to work harder to understand the entire passage's message.

Figure 11: Example of How Use of Inappropriate Emphasis Reduces Readability in Typical Credit Card Disclosure Documents

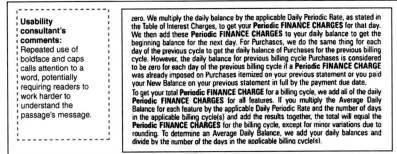

Usability consultant's comments: Repeated use of boldface and caps calls attention to a word, potentially requiring readers to work harder to understand the passage's message.

zero. We multiply the daily balance by the applicable Daily Periodic Rate, as stated in the Table of Interest Charges, to get your **Periodic FINANCE CHARGES** for that day. We then add these **Periodic FINANCE CHARGES** to your daily balance to get the beginning balance for the next day. For Purchases, we do the same thing for each day of the previous cycle to get the daily balance of Purchases for the previous billing cycle. However, the daily balance for previous billing cycle Purchases is considered to be zero for each day of the previous billing cycle if a **Periodic FINANCE CHARGE** was already imposed on Purchases itemized on your previous statement or you paid your New Balance on your previous statement in full by the payment due date.

To get your total **Periodic FINANCE CHARGE** for a billing cycle, we add all of the daily **Periodic FINANCE CHARGES** for all features. If you multiply the Average Daily Balance for each feature by the applicable Daily Periodic Rate and the number of days in the applicable billing cycle(s) and add the results together, the total will equal the **Periodic FINANCE CHARGES** for the billing cycle, except for minor variations due to rounding. To determine an Average Daily Balance, we add your daily balances and divide by the number of the days in the applicable billing cycle(s).

Sources: UserWorks, Inc.; Information International Associates.

- *Use of headings.* According to the usability consultant, disclosure documents from three of the four issuers analyzed contained headings that were difficult to distinguish from surrounding text. Headings, according to the consultant, provide a visual hierarchy to help readers quickly identify information in a lengthy document. Good headers are easy to identify and use meaningful labels. Figure 12 illustrates two examples of how the credit card disclosure documents failed to use headings effectively.

Figure 12: Example of Ineffective and Effective Use of Headings in Typical Credit Card Disclosure Documents

Ineffective heading use (shading added by GAO)

Section 2: USE OF YOUR ACCOUNT
2.1: Types of Transactions. You may use your Account for the following types of consumer transactions:
   2.1.1: Purchases. Purchase goods or services with your Card.
   2.1.2: Cash Advances. Obtain cash from a participating financial institution or merchant ("Cash Disbursement") or from an ATM ("ATM Advance"), write a Convenience Check for any legal purpose ("Convenience Check Advance") or purchase money orders, travelers checks, foreign currency, lottery tickets, casino chips, racetrack wagers, vouchers redeemable for cash or other items readily convertible into cash ("Quasi Cash"), or transfer funds from your Account to your   personal checking account for overdraft protection ("Overdraft Protection").
   2.1.3: Balance Transfers. Transferred balances to your Account from other creditors, except those made using a Convenience Check.
2.2: Limitations on Use

(1)

Payment Allocation: You agree that we are authorized to allocate your payments and credits in a way that is most favorable to or convenient for us. For example, you authorize us to apply your payments and credits to balances with lower **Annual Percentage Rates** ("APRs") (such as promotional APRs) before balances with higher APRs for all balances except promotional balances for Disney vacation packages.

Credit Line/Authorized Usage: Your credit line is shown on the folder containing your Card. Since we may change your credit line from time to time, your latest credit line will appear on your monthly statement. You agree not to make a Purchase or obtain a Cash Advance that would cause the unpaid balance of your Account to exceed your

(2)

Effective heading use (shading added by GAO)

(3) *How We Determine the Balance:*
The total outstanding balance (the amount you owe us) appears as the "New Balance" on the billing statement. To determine the New Balance, we begin with the outstanding balance on your account at the beginning of each billing period, called the "Previous Balance" on the billing statement. We add any purchases or cash advances and subtract any credits or payments credited as of that billing period. We then add the appropriate finance charges and fees and make other applicable adjustments.

Annual Percentage Rates for Purchases and Cash Advances:
Your annual percentage rates and the corresponding daily periodic rates appear on the card carrier. A daily periodic rate is the appli-

Usability consultant's comments:

(1) Headings are easy to identify, but are preceded by an unnecessary string of numbers that do not correspond to anything useful like a table of contents.

(2) Headings are not substantially different from the text.

Usability consultant's comments:

(3) Headings are easy to distinguish from the surrounding text.

Sources: UserWorks, Inc.; Information International Associates.

In the first example, the headings contained an unnecessary string of numbers that the consultant found would make locating a specific topic in the text more difficult. As a result, readers would need to actively ignore the string of numbers until the middle of the line to find what they wanted. The consultant noted that such numbers might be useful if this document had a table of contents that referred to the numbers, but it did not. In the second example, the consultant noted that a reader's ability to locate information using the headings in this document was hindered because the headings were not made more visually distinct, but instead were aligned with other text and printed in the same type size as the text that followed. As a result, these headings blended in with the text. Furthermore, the consultant noted that because the term "Annual Percentage Rates" was given the same visual treatment as the two headings in the example, finding headings quickly was made even more difficult. In contrast, figure 12 also shows an example that the consultant identified in one of the disclosure documents that was an effective use of headings.

- *Presentation techniques.* According to the usability consultant, the disclosure documents analyzed did not use presentation techniques, such as tables, bulleted lists, and graphics, that could help to simplify the presentation of complicated concepts, especially in the cardmember agreements. Best practices for document design suggest using tables and bulleted lists to simplify the presentation of complex information. Instead, the usability consultant noted that all the cardmember agreements reviewed almost exclusively employed undifferentiated blocks of text, potentially hindering clear communication of complex information, such as the multiple-step procedures issuers use for calculating a cardholder's minimum required payment. Figure 13 below presents two samples of text from different cardmember agreements describing how minimum payments are calculated. According to the consultant, the sample that used a bulleted list was easier to read than the one formatted as a paragraph. Also, an issuer stated in a letter to the Federal Reserve that their consumers have welcomed the issuer's use of bullets to format information, emphasizing the concept that the visual layout of information either facilitates or hinders consumer understanding.

Figure 13: Example of How Presentation Techniques Can Affect Readability in Typical Credit Card Disclosure Documents

<table>
<tr>
<td>

MINIMUM MONTHLY PAYMENT. The Minimum Payment Due each month will be the sum of any amount past due and the minimum monthly payment. The minimum monthly payment each month will be the greater of $10 or 1/50th of the New Balance, rounded to the next higher whole dollar amount. If any ANNUAL PERCENTAGE RATE applicable to your Account is greater than 22.99%, but less than 26.00%, your minimum monthly payment will be the greater of $10 or 1/45th of the New Balance, rounded to the next higher whole dollar amount. If any ANNUAL PERCENTAGE RATE applicable to your Account is 26.00% or greater, your minimum monthly payment will be the greater of $10 or 1/40th of the New Balance. Regardless of the Annual Percentage Rates on your Account, if the New Balance is less than $10.00, the minimum monthly payment will be the amount of the New Balance. We may also include in your minimum monthly payment all or a portion of the amount by which your outstanding balance exceeds your Account credit limit as of the last day of the billing period. Paying the Minimum Payment Due may be insufficient to bring

</td>
<td>

Minimum Amount Due:
Each month you must pay a minimum amount that is calculated as follows. First, we begin with any amount that is past due and add to it any amount in excess of your credit line. Second, we add the largest of the following:

• The New Balance on the billing statement if it is less than $20;

• $20 if the New Balance is at least $20;

• 1% of the New Balance (which calculation is rounded down to the nearest dollar) plus the amount of your billed finance charges and any applicable late fee; or

• 1.5% of the New Balance (which calculation is rounded down to the nearest dollar).

However, the Minimum Amount Due will never exceed your New Balance. In calculating the Minimum Amount Due, we may subtract from the New Balance certain fees added to your account during the billing period.

</td>
</tr>
<tr>
<td>

Usability consultant's comments:
Expressing a complicated, multistep process as prose makes it difficult to understand the relationships between steps.

</td>
<td>

Usability consultant's comments:
By using bullet points, it is much easier to see multiple steps broken out into individual steps and when they are applied.

</td>
</tr>
</table>

Sources: UserWorks, Inc.; Information International Associates.

Excessive Complexity and Volume of Information

The content of typical credit card disclosure documents generally was overly complex and presented in too much detail, such as by using unfamiliar or complex terms to describe simple concepts. For example, the usability consultant identified one cardmember agreement that used the term "rolling consecutive twelve billing cycle period" instead of saying "over the course of the next 12 billing statements" or "next 12 months"—if that was appropriate. Further, a number of consumers, consumer advocacy groups, and government and private entities that have provided comments to the Federal Reserve agreed that typical credit card disclosures are written in complex language that hinders consumers' understanding. For example, a consumer wrote that disclosure documents were "loaded with booby traps designed to trip consumers, and written in intentionally impenetrable and confusing language." One of the consumer advocacy groups stated the disclosures were "full of dense, impenetrable legal jargon that even lawyers and seasoned consumer advocates have difficulty understanding." In addition, the consultant noted that many of the disclosures, including solicitation letters and cardmember agreements, contained overly long and complex sentences that increase the effort a reader must devote to understanding the text. Figure 14 contains two examples of instances in which the disclosure documents used uncommon words and phrases to express simple concepts.

Figure 14: Examples of How Removing Overly Complex Language Can Improve Readability in Typical Credit Card Disclosure Documents

101 words	*¹If at any time during any rolling consecutive twelve billing cycle period you fail to make two Minimum Payments on a timely basis or exceed your Credit Limit twice we may elect to increase your Purchase, Cash Advance and/or Balance Transfer APRs to the Penalty APRs. All Penalty APRs will remain in effect until, in a subsequent rolling consecutive six billing cycle period, you do not exceed your Credit Limit at any time and you make all of your required Minimum Payments on a timely basis when, in your next billing cycle, all Penalty APRs will no longer apply.*
50 words	**Usability consultant's rewrite:** If you pay late or go over your credit limit twice in a year, the interest rate you pay on most things goes up to the default rate, currently 30.49%. It will go back down when you pay on time and do not go over your credit limit for six months.
69 words	**Using Your Account:** You may use your Card or Account to purchase or lease goods or services, or pay amounts you owe, wherever the Card is honored, transfer balances from other accounts or, if applicable, to obtain advances to cover an overdraft on your checking account with a affiliate under the terms of this Agreement and your Overdraft Protection Agreement, ("Overdraft Advances"), (Purchases, Balance Transfers and Overdraft Advances are collectively called "Purchases").
20 words	**Usability consultant's rewrite:** You can use this card to buy things, pay off other accounts, transfer balances, or keep from bouncing a check.

Sources: UserWorks, Inc.; Information International Associates.

In addition, the disclosure documents regularly presented too much or irrelevant detail. According to the usability consultant's analysis, the credit card disclosures often contained superfluous information. For example, figure 15 presents an example of text from one cardmember agreement that described the actions the issuer would take if its normal source for the rate information used to set its variable rates—*The Wall Street Journal*—were to cease publication. Including such an arguably unimportant detail lengthens and makes this disclosure more complex. According to SEC best practices for creating clear disclosures, disclosure documents are more effective when they adhere to the rule that less is more. By omitting unnecessary details from disclosure documents, the usability consultant indicated that consumers would be more likely to read and understand the information they contain.

Figure 15: Example of Superfluous Detail in Typical Credit Card Disclosure Documents

Usability consultant's comments: This section provides superfluous information on how the prime rate is determined. For example, the explanation of the actions if the Wall Street Journal was to cease publication.	If any annual percentage rate is based on the U.S. Prime Rate plus a margin, we will calculate the rate for each billing period by adding the applicable margin that appears on the card carrier to the U.S. Prime Rate. For each billing period we will use the U.S. Prime Rate published in *The Wall Street Journal* two business days prior to your Statement/Closing Date for that billing period. Any increase or decrease in a variable annual percentage rate due to a change in the U.S. Prime Rate takes effect as of the first day of the billing period for which we calculate the variable annual percentage rate. If more than one U.S. Prime Rate is published, we may choose the highest rate. If *The Wall Street Journal* ceases publication or to publish the U.S. Prime Rate, we may use the U.S. Prime Rate published in any other newspaper of general circulation, or we may substitute a similar reference rate at our sole discretion. When a change in an applicable variable annual percentage rate takes effect we will apply it to any existing balances, subject to any promotional rate that may apply.

Sources: UserWorks, Inc.; Information International Associates.

Consumer Confusion Indicated That Disclosures Were Not Communicating Credit Card Cost Information Clearly

Many of the credit cardholders that were tested and interviewed as part of our review exhibited confusion over various fees, practices, and other terms that could affect the cost of using their credit cards. To understand how well consumers could use typical credit card disclosure documents to locate and understand information about card fees and other practices, the usability consultant with whom we contracted used a sample of cardholders to perform a usability assessment of the disclosure documents from the four large issuers. As part of this assessment, the consultant conducted one-on-one sessions with a total of 12 cardholders so that each set of disclosures, which included a solicitation letter and a cardmember agreement, was reviewed by 3 cardholders.[51] Each of these cardholders were asked to locate information about fee levels and rates, the circumstances in which they would be imposed, and information about changes in card terms. The consultant also tested the cardholders' ability to explain various practices used by the issuer, such as the process for determining the amount of the minimum monthly payment, by reading the disclosure documents. Although the results of the usability testing cannot

---

[51]According to the consultant, testing with small numbers of individuals can generally identify many of the problems that can affect the readability and usability of materials.

be used to make generalizations about all cardholders, the consultant selected cardholders based on the demographics of the U.S. adult population, according to age, education level, and income, to ensure that the cardholders tested were representative of the general population. In addition, as part of this review, we conducted one-on-one interviews with 112 cardholders to learn about consumer behavior and knowledge about various credit card terms and practices.[52] Although we also selected these cardholders to reflect the demographics of the U.S. adult population, with respect to age, education level, and income, the results of these interviews cannot be generalized to the population of all U.S. cardholders.[53]

Based on the work with consumers, specific aspects of credit card terms that apparently were not well understood included:

- *Default interest rates.* Although issuers can penalize cardholders for violating the terms of the card, such as by making late payments or by increasing the interest rates in effect on the cardholder's account to rates as high as 30 percent or more, only about half of the cardholders that the usability consultant tested were able to use the typical credit card disclosure documents to successfully identify the default rate and the circumstances that would trigger rate increases for these cards. In addition, the usability consultant observed the cardholders could not identify this information easily. Many also were unsure of their answers, especially when rates were expressed as a "prime plus" number, indicating the rate varied based on the prime rate. Locating information in the typical cardmember agreement was especially difficult for cardholders, as only 3 of 12 cardholders were able to use such documents to identify the default interest rate applicable to the card. More importantly, only about half of the cardholders tested using solicitation letters were able to accurately determine what actions could potentially cause the default rate to be imposed on these cards.

- *Other penalty rate increases.* Although card issuers generally reserve the right to seek to raise a cardholder's rate in other situations, such as when a cardholder makes a late payment to another issuer's credit card, (even if the cardholder has not defaulted on the cardmember

---

[52]We also used this data in a previous report to show cardholder preferences for customized information in their monthly billing statements about the consequences of making minimum payments on their outstanding balance. GAO-06-434.

[53]For more information about our scope and methodology, see appendix I.

agreement), about 71 percent of the 112 cardholders we interviewed were unsure or did not believe that issuers could increase their rates in such a case. In addition, about two-thirds of cardholders we interviewed were unaware or did not believe that a drop in their credit score could cause an issuer to seek to assess higher interest rates on their account.[54]

- *Late payment fees.* According to the usability assessment, many of the cardholders had trouble using the disclosure documents to correctly identify what would occur if a payment were to be received after the due date printed in the billing statement. For example, nearly half of the cardholders were unable to use the cardmember agreement to determine whether a payment would be considered late based on the date the issuer receives the payment or the date the payment was mailed or postmarked. Additionally, the majority of the 112 cardholders we interviewed also exhibited confusion over late fees: 52 percent indicated that they have been surprised when their card company applied a fee or penalty to their account.

- *Using a credit card to obtain cash.* Although the cardholders tested by the consultant generally were able to use the disclosures to identify how a transaction fee for a cash advance would be calculated, most were unable to accurately use this information to determine the transaction fee for withdrawing funds, usually because they neglected to consider the minimum dollar amount, such as $5 or $10, that would be assessed.

- *Grace periods.* Almost all 12 cardholders in the usability assessment had trouble using the solicitation letters to locate and define the grace period, the period during which the a cardholder is not charged interest on a balance. Instead, many cardholders incorrectly indicated that the grace period was instead when their lower, promotional interest rates would expire. Others incorrectly indicated that it was the amount of time after the monthly bill's due date that a cardholder could submit a payment without being charged a late fee.

- *Balance computation method.* Issuers use various methods to calculate interest charges on outstanding balances, but only 1 of the 12 cardholders the usability consultant tested correctly described average

---

[54]A credit score is a number, roughly between 300 and 800, that reflects the credit history detailed by a person's credit report. Lenders use borrowers' credit scores in the process of assigning rates and terms to the loans they make.

daily balance, and none of the cardholders were able to describe two-cycle average daily balance accurately. At least nine letters submitted to the Federal Reserve in connection with its review of credit card disclosures noted that few consumers understand balance computation methods as stated in disclosure documents.

Perhaps as a result of weaknesses previously described, cardholders generally avoid using the documents issuers provide with a new card to improve their understanding of fees and practices. For example, many of the cardholders interviewed as part of this report noted that the length, format, and complexity of disclosures led them to generally disregard the information contained in them. More than half (54 percent) of the 112 cardholders we interviewed indicated they read the disclosures provided with a new card either not very closely or not at all. Instead, many cardholders said they would call the issuer's customer service representatives for information about their card's terms and conditions. Cardholders also noted that the ability of issuers to change the terms and conditions of a card at any time led them to generally disregard the information contained in card disclosures. Regulation Z allows card issuers to change the terms of credit cards provided that issuers notify cardholders in writing within 15 days of the change. As a result, the usability consultant observed some participants were dismissive of the information in the disclosure documents because they were aware that issuers could change anything.

Federal Reserve Effort to Revise Regulations Presents Opportunity to Improve Disclosures

With liability concerns and outdated regulatory requirements seemingly explaining the weaknesses in card disclosures, the Federal Reserve has begun efforts to review its requirements for credit card disclosures. Industry participants have advocated various ways in which the Federal Reserve can act to improve these disclosures and otherwise assist cardholders.

Regulations and Guidance May Contribute to Weaknesses in Current Disclosures

Several factors may help explain why typical credit card disclosures exhibit weaknesses that reduce their usefulness to cardholders. First, issuers make decisions about the content and format of their disclosures to limit potential legal liability. Issuer representatives told us that the disclosures made in credit card solicitations and cardmember agreements are written for legal purposes and in language that consumers generally could not understand. For example, representatives for one large issuer told us they cannot always state information in disclosures clearly because the increased potential that simpler statements would be misinterpreted would expose them to litigation. Similarly, a participant of a symposium on credit card disclosures said that disclosures typically became lengthier after the issuance of court rulings on consumer credit issues. Issuers can attempt to reduce the risk of civil liability based on their disclosures by closely following the formats that the Federal Reserve has provided in its model forms and other guidance. According to the regulations that govern card disclosures, issuers acting in good faith compliance with any interpretation issued by a duly authorized official or employee of the Federal Reserve are afforded protection from liability.[55]

Second, the regulations governing credit card disclosures have become outdated. As noted earlier in this report, TILA and Regulation Z that implements the act's provisions are intended to ensure that consumers have adequate information about potential costs and other applicable terms and conditions to make appropriate choices among competing credit cards. The most recent comprehensive revisions to Regulation Z's open-end credit rules occurred in 1989 to implement the provisions of the Fair Credit and Charge Card Act. As we have found, the features and cost structures of credit cards have changed considerably since then. An issuer representative told us that current Schumer box requirements are not as useful in presenting the more complicated structures of many current cards. For example, they noted that it does not easily accommodate information about the various cardholder actions that could trigger rate increases, which they argued is now important information for consumers to know when shopping for credit. As a result, some of the specific requirements of Regulation Z that are intended to ensure that consumers have accurate information instead may be diminishing the usefulness of these disclosures.

Third, the guidance that the Federal Reserve provides issuers may not be consistent with guidelines for producing clear, written documents. Based on our analysis, many issuers appear to adhere to the formats and model forms that the Federal Reserve staff included in the Official Staff Interpretations of Regulation Z, which are prepared to help issuers comply with the regulations. For example, the model forms present text about how rates are determined in footnotes. However, as discussed previously, not grouping related information undermines the usability of documents. The

---

[55]Under Section 130(f) of the TILA, creditors are protected from civil liability for any act done or omitted in good faith in conformity with any interpretation issued by a duly authorized official or employee of the Federal Reserve System. 15 U.S.C. § 1640.

Schumer box format requires a cardholder to look in several places, such as in multiple rows in the table and in notes to the table, for information about related aspects of the card. Similarly, the Federal Reserve's model form for the Schumer box recommends that the information about the transaction fee and interest rate for cash advances be disclosed in different areas.

Finally, the way that issuers have implemented regulatory guidance may have contributed to the weaknesses typical disclosure materials exhibited. For example, in certain required disclosures, the terms "annual percentage rate" and "finance charge," when used with a corresponding amount or percentage rate, are required to be more conspicuous than any other required disclosures.[56] Staff guidance suggests that such terms may be made more conspicuous by, for example, capitalizing these terms when other disclosures are printed in lower case or by displaying these terms in larger type relative to other disclosures, putting them in boldface print or underlining them.[57] Our usability consultant's analysis found that card disclosure documents that followed this guidance were less effective because they placed an inappropriate emphasis on terms. As shown previously in figure 11, the use of bold and capital letters to emphasize the term "finance charge" in the paragraph unnecessarily calls attention to that term, potentially distracting readers from information that is more important. The excerpt shown in figure 11 is from an initial disclosure document which, according to Regulation Z, is subject to the "more conspicuous" rule requiring emphasis of the terms "finance charge" and "annual percentage rate."

Suggestions for Improving Disclosures Included Obtaining Input from Consumers

With the intention of improving credit card disclosures, the Federal Reserve has begun efforts to develop new regulations. According to its 2004 notice seeking public comments on Regulation Z, the Federal Reserve hopes to address the length, complexity, and superfluous information of disclosures and produce new disclosures that will be more useful in helping consumers compare credit products.[58] After the passage of the

---

[56]See generally 12 C.F.R. 225.5(a)(3) and the corresponding staff commentary.

[57]Notwithstanding the more conspicuous rule, Regulation Z expressly provides that the annual percentage rate for purchases required to be disclosed in the Schumer box must be in at least 18-point type. 12 C.F.R. § 226.5a(b)(1).

[58]Truth in Lending, 69 Fed. Reg. 70925 (advanced notice of proposed rulemaking, published Dec. 8, 2004).

Bankruptcy Abuse Prevention and Consumer Protection Act of 2005 (Bankruptcy Act) in October of that year, which included amendments to TILA, the Federal Reserve sought additional comments from the public to prepare to implement new disclosure requirements including disclosures intended to advise consumers of the consequences of making only minimum payments on credit cards.[59] According to Federal Reserve staff, new credit card disclosure regulations may not be in effect until sometime in 2007 or 2008 because of the time required to conduct consumer testing, modify the existing regulations, and then seek comment on the revised regulation.

Industry participants and others have provided input to assist the Federal Reserve in this effort. Based on the interviews we conducted, documents we reviewed, and our analysis of the more than 280 comment letters submitted to the Federal Reserve, issuers, consumer groups, and others provided various suggestions to improve the content and format of credit card disclosures, including:

- *Reduce the amount of information disclosed.* Some industry participants said that some of the information currently presented in the Schumer box could be removed because it is too complicated to disclose meaningfully or otherwise lacks importance compared to other credit terms that are arguably more important when choosing among cards. Such information included the method for computing balances and the amount of the minimum finance charge (the latter because it is typically so small, about 50 cents in 2005).

- *Provide a shorter document that summarizes key information.* Some industry participants advocated that all key information that could significantly affect a cardholder's costs be presented in a short document that consumers could use to readily compare across cards, with all other details included in a longer document. For example, although the Schumer box includes several key pieces of information, it does not include other information that could be as important for consumer decisions, such as what actions could cause the issuer to raise the interest rate to the default rate.

---

[59]Truth in Lending, 70 Fed. Reg. 60235 (request for comments; extension of comment period, published October 17, 2005).

- *Revise disclosure formats to improve readability.* Various suggestions were made to improve the readability of card disclosures, including making more use of tables of contents, making labels and headings more prominent, and presenting more information in tables instead of in text. Disclosure documents also could use consistent wording that could allow for better comparison of terms across cards.

Some issuers and others also told us that the new regulations should allow for more flexibility in card disclosure formats. Regulations mandating formats and font sizes were seen as precluding issuers from presenting information in more effective ways. For example, one issuer already has conducted market research and developed new formats for the Schumer box that it says are more readable and contain new information important to choosing cards in today's credit card environment, such as cardholder actions that would trigger late fees or penalty interest rate increases.

In addition to suggestions about content, obtaining the input of consumers, and possibly other professionals, was also seen as an important way to make any new disclosures more useful. For example, participants in a Federal Reserve Bank symposium on credit card disclosures recommended that the Federal Reserve obtain the input of marketers, researchers, and consumers as part of developing new disclosures. OCC staff suggested that the Federal Reserve also employ qualitative research methods such as in-depth interviews with consumers and others and that it conduct usability testing.

Consumer testing can validate the effectiveness or measure the comprehension of messages and information, and detect document design problems. Many issuers are using some form of market research to test their disclosure materials and have advocated improving disclosures by seeking the input of marketers, researchers, and consumers.[60] SEC also has recently used consumer focus groups to test the format of new disclosures related to mutual funds. According to an SEC staff member who participated in this effort, their testing provided them with valuable information on what consumers liked and disliked about some of the initial forms that the regulator had drafted. In some cases, they learned that

---

[60]Consumer testing can be conducted in several ways, such as focus groups, where consumers analyze products in a group setting, and conjoint analysis, which helps companies understand the extent to which consumers prefer certain product attributes over others.

information that SEC staff had considered necessary to include was not seen as important by consumers. As a result, they revised the formats for these disclosures substantially to make them simpler and may use graphics to present more information rather than text.[61] According to Federal Reserve staff, they have begun to involve consumers in the development of new credit card disclosures. According to Federal Reserve staff, they have already conducted some consumer focus groups. In addition, they have contracted with a design consultant and a market research firm to help them develop some disclosure formats that they can then use in one-on-one testing with consumers. However, the Federal Reserve staff told us they recognize the challenge of designing disclosures that include all key information in a clear manner, given the complexity of credit card products and the different ways in which consumers use credit cards.

Although Credit Card Penalty Fees and Interest Could Increase Indebtedness, the Extent to Which They Have Contributed to Bankruptcies Was Unclear

The number of consumers filing for bankruptcy has risen more than six-fold over the past 25 years, and various factors have been cited as possible explanations. While some researchers have pointed to increases in total debt or credit card debt in particular, others found that debt burdens and other measures of financial distress had not increased and thus cite other factors, such as a general decline in the stigma of going bankrupt or the potentially increased costs of major life events such as health problems or divorce. Some critics of the credit card industry have cited penalty interest and fees as leading to increased financial distress; however, no comprehensive data existed to determine the extent to which these charges were contributing to consumer bankruptcies. Data provided by the six largest card issuers indicated that unpaid interest and fees represented a small portion of the amounts owed by cardholders that filed for bankruptcy; however, these data alone were not sufficient to determine any relationship between the charges and bankruptcies filed by cardholders.

Researchers Cited Various Factors as Explanations for Rise in Consumer Bankruptcies

According to U.S. Department of Justice statistics, consumer bankruptcy filings generally rose steadily from about 287,000 in 1980 to more than 2 million as of December 31, 2005, which represents about a 609 percent

---

[61]Securities Exchange Act Release No. 33-8544 (Feb. 28, 2005).

increase over the last 25 years.[62] Researchers have cited a number of factors as possible explanations for the long-term trend.

Increase in Household Indebtedness

The total debt of American households is composed of mortgages on real estate, which accounts for about 80 percent of the total, and consumer credit debt, which includes revolving credit, such as balances owed on credit cards, and nonrevolving credit, primarily consisting of auto loans. According to Federal Reserve statistics, consumers' use of debt has expanded over the last 25 years, increasing more than sevenfold from $1.4 trillion in 1980 to about $11.5 trillion in 2005. Some researchers pointed to this rise in overall indebtedness as contributing to the rise in bankruptcies. For example, a 2000 Congressional Budget Office summary of bankruptcy research noted that various academic studies have argued that consumer bankruptcies are either directly or indirectly caused by heavy consumer indebtedness.

Rather than total debt, some researchers and others argue that the rise in bankruptcies is related to the rise in credit card debt in particular. According to the Federal Reserve's survey of consumer debt, the amount of credit card debt reported as outstanding rose from about $237 billion to more than $802 billion—a 238 percent increase between 1990 and 2005.[63] One academic researcher noted that the rise in bankruptcies and charge-offs by banks in credit card accounts grew along with the increase in credit card debt during the 1973 to 1996 period he examined.[64] According to some consumer groups, the growth of credit card debt is one of the primary explanations of the increased prevalence of bankruptcies in the United States. For example, one group noted in a 2005 testimony before Congress that growth of credit card debt—particularly among lower and moderate income households, consumers with poor credit scores, college students,

[62]Bankruptcy filings sharply increased recently, with filings in 2005 30 percent higher than in 2004. This increase likely resulted from the accelerated rate of filing that occurred in the months before the new Bankruptcy Abuse Prevention and Consumer Protection Act of 2005, which tightened eligibility for filing, became effective on October 17, 2005.

[63]In addition to capturing amounts outstanding on credit cards, the number reported in the Federal Reserve's survey of consumer debt for revolving debt also includes other types of revolving debt. However, Federal Reserve staff familiar with the survey's results indicated that the vast majority of the amount reported as revolving debt is from credit cards.

[64]L. Ausubel, "Credit Card Defaults, Credit Card Profits, and Bankruptcy," *The American Bankruptcy Law Journal*, 71 (Spring 1997).

older Americans, and minorities—was contributing to the rise in bankruptcies.[65]

However, other evidence indicates that increased indebtedness has not severely affected the financial condition of U.S. households in general. For example:

- Some researchers note that the ability of households to make payments on debt appears to be keeping pace. For example, total household debt levels as a percentage of income has remained relatively constant since the 1980s. According to the Federal Reserve, the aggregate debt burden ratio—which covers monthly aggregate required payments of all households on mortgage debt and both revolving and non-revolving consumer loans relative to the aggregate monthly disposable income of all households—for U.S. households has been above 13 percent in the last few years but generally fluctuated between 11 percent and 14 percent from 1990 to 2005, similar to the levels observed during the 1980s. According to one researcher, although the debt burden ratio has risen since the 1980s, the increase has been gradual and therefore cannot explain the six-fold increase in consumer bankruptcy filings over the same period.

- Credit card debt remains a small portion of overall household debt, even among households with the lowest income levels. According to the Federal Reserve, credit card balances as a percentage of total household debt have declined from 3.9 percent of total household debt in 1995 to just 3.0 percent as of 2004.

- The proportion of households that could be considered to be in financial distress does not appear to be increasing significantly. According to the Federal Reserve Board's Survey of Consumer Finances, the proportion of households that could be considered to be in financial distress— those that report debt-to-income ratios exceeding 40 percent and that have had at least one delinquent payment within the last 60 days—was relatively stable between 1995 and 2004. Further, the proportion of the

---

[65]Consumer Federation of America testimony before the Committee on Banking, Housing, and Urban Affairs of the United States Senate, *"Examining the Current Legal and Regulatory Requirements and Industry Practices for Credit Card Issuers with Respect to Consumer Disclosures and Marketing Efforts,"* 109th Congress, 2nd sess., May 17, 2005. We reported on issues relating to college students and credits in 2001. See GAO, *Consumer Finance: College Students and Credit Cards*, GAO-01-773 (Washington, D.C.; June 20, 2001).

lowest-income households exhibiting greater levels of distress was lower in 2004 than it was in the 1990s.

Other Explanations

With the effect of increased debt unclear, some researchers say that other factors may better explain the surge in consumer bankruptcy filings over the past 25 years. For example, the psychological stigma of declaring bankruptcy may have lessened. One academic study examined a range of variables that measured the credit risk (risk of default) of several hundred thousand credit card accounts and found that because the bankruptcy rate for the accounts was higher than the credit-risk variables could explain, the higher rate must be the result of a reduced level of stigma associated with filing.[66] However, others have noted that reliably measuring stigma is difficult. Some credit card issuers and other industry associations also have argued that the pre-2005 bankruptcy code was too debtor-friendly and created an incentive for consumers to borrow beyond the ability to repay and file for bankruptcy.

In addition to the possibly reduced stigma, some academics, consumer advocacy groups, and others noted that the normal life events that reduce incomes or increase expenses for households may have a more serious effect today. Events that can reduce household incomes include job losses, pay cuts, or having a full-time position converted to part-time work. With increasing health care costs, medical emergencies can affect household expenses and debts more significantly than in the past, and, with more families relying on two incomes, so can divorces. As a result, one researcher explains that while these risks have always faced households, their effect today may be more severe, which could explain higher bankruptcy rates.[67]

Researchers who assert that life events are the primary explanation for bankruptcy filings say that the role played by credit cards can vary. They acknowledged that credit card debt can be a contributing factor to a bankruptcy filing if a person's income is insufficient to meet all financial obligations, including payments to credit card issuers. For example, some individuals experiencing an adverse life event use credit cards to provide

---

[66]David B. Gross and Nicholas S. Souleles, "Explaining the Increase in Bankruptcy and Delinquency: Stigma Versus Risk-Composition." Mimeo, University of Chicago, (August 28, 1998).

[67]Elizabeth Warren, Leo Gottlieb Professor of Law, Harvard Law School, "The Growing Threat to Middle Class Families," *Brooklyn Law Review*, (April 2003).

additional funds to satisfy their financial obligations temporarily but ultimately exhaust their ability to meet all obligations. However, because the number of people that experience financially troublesome life events likely exceeds the number of people who file for bankruptcy, credit cards in other cases may serve as a critical temporary source of funding they needed to avert a filing until that person's income recovers or expenses diminish. (Appendix II provides additional detail about the factors that may have affected the rise in consumer bankruptcy filings and its relationship with credit card debt.)

The Extent to Which Credit Card Penalty Interest and Fees Contribute to Consumer Bankruptcies Remains Controversial in the Absence of Comprehensive Data

With very little information available on the financial condition of individuals filing for bankruptcy, assessing the role played by credit card debt, including penalty interest and fees, is difficult. According to Department of Justice officials who oversee bankruptcy trustees in most bankruptcy courts, the documents submitted as part of a bankruptcy filing show the total debt owed to each card issuer but not how much of this total consists of unpaid principal, interest, or fees. Similarly, these Justice officials told us that the information that credit card issuers submit when their customers reaffirm the debts owed to them—known as proofs of claim—also indicate only the total amount owed. Likewise, the amount of any penalty interest or fees owed as part of an outstanding credit card balance is generally not required to be specified when a credit card issuer seeks to obtain a court judgment that would require payment from a customer as part of a collection case.

Opinions on the Link between Credit Card Practices and Bankruptcies Vary

Although little comprehensive data exist, some consumer groups and others have argued that penalty interest and fees materially harm the financial condition of some cardholders, including those that later file for bankruptcy. Some researchers who study credit card issues argue that high interest rates (applicable to standard purchases) for higher risk cardholders, who are also frequently lower-income households, along with penalty and default interest rates and fees, contribute to more consumer bankruptcy filings. Another researcher who has studied issues relating to credit cards and bankruptcy asserted that consumers focus too much on the introductory purchase interest rates when shopping for credit cards and, as a result, fail to pay close attention to penalty interest rates, default clauses, and other fees that may significantly increase their costs later. According to this researcher, it is doubtful that penalty fees (such as late fees and over-limit fees) significantly affect cardholders' debt levels, but accrued interest charges—particularly if a cardholder is being assessed a high penalty interest rate—can significantly worsen a cardholder's financial distress.

Some consumer advocacy groups and academics say that the credit card industry practice of raising cardholder interest rates for default or increased risky behavior likely has contributed to some consumer bankruptcy filings. According to these groups, cardholders whose rates are raised under such practices can find it more difficult to reduce their credit card debt and experience more rapid declines in their overall financial conditions as they struggle to make the higher payments that such interest rates may entail. As noted earlier in this report, card issuers have generally ceased practicing universal default, although representatives for four of the six issuers told us that they might increase their cardholder's rates if they saw indications that the cardholder's risk has increased, such as how well they were making payments to other creditors. In such cases, the card issuers said they notify the cardholders in advance, by sending a change in terms notice, and provide an option to cancel the account but keep the original terms and conditions while paying off the balance.

Some organizations also have criticized the credit card industry for targeting lower-income households that they believe may be more likely to experience financial distress or file for bankruptcy. One of the criticisms these organizations have made is that credit card companies have been engaging in bottom-fishing by providing increasing amounts of credit to riskier lower-income households that, as a result, may incur greater levels of indebtedness than appropriate. For example, an official from one consumer advocacy group testified in 2005 that card issuers target lower-income and minority households and that this democratization of credit has had serious negative consequences for these households, placing them one financial emergency away from having to file for bankruptcy.[68] Some consumer advocacy group officials and academics noted that card issuers market high-cost cards, with higher interest rates and fees, to customers with poor credit histories—called subprime customers—including some just coming out of bankruptcy. However, as noted earlier, Federal Reserve survey data indicate that the proportion of lower-income households— those with incomes below the fortieth percentile—exhibiting financial distress has not increased since 1995. In addition, in a June 2006 report that the Federal Reserve Board prepared for Congress on the relationship

---

[68]See above: Consumer Federation of America testimony before the Committee on Banking, Housing, and Urban Affairs of the United States Senate on May 17, 2005.

between credit cards and bankruptcy, it stated that credit card issuers do not solicit customers or extend credit to them indiscriminately or without assessing their ability to repay debt as issuers review all received applications for risk factors.[69]

In addition, representatives of credit card issuers argued that they do not offer credit to those likely to become financially bankrupt because they do not want to experience larger losses from higher-risk borrowers. Because card accounts belonging to cardholders that filed for bankruptcy account for a sizeable portion of issuers' charge-offs, card issuers do not want to acquire new customers with high credit risk who may subsequently file for bankruptcy. However, one academic researcher noted that, if card issuers could increase their revenue and profits by offering cards to more customers, including those with lower creditworthiness, they could reasonably be expected to do so until the amount of expected losses from bankruptcies becomes larger than the expected additional revenues from the new customers.

In examining the relationship between the consumer credit industry and bankruptcy, the Federal Reserve Board's 2006 report comes to many of the same conclusions as the studies of other researchers we reviewed. The Federal Reserve Board's report notes that despite large growth in the proportion of households with credit cards and the rise in overall credit card debt in recent decades, the debt-burden ratio and other potential measures of financial distress have not significantly changed over this period. The report also found that, while data on bankruptcy filings indicate that most filers have accumulated consumer debt and the proportion of filings and rise in revolving consumer debt have risen in tandem, the decision to file for bankruptcy is complex and tends to be driven by distress arising from life events such as job loss, divorce, or uninsured illness.

Penalty Interest and Fees Can Affect Cardholders' Ability to Reduce Outstanding Balances

While the effect of credit card penalty interest charges and fees on consumer bankruptcies was unclear, such charges do reduce the ability of cardholders to reduce their overall indebtedness. Generally, any penalty charges that cardholders pay would consume funds that could have been used to repay principal. Figure 16 below, compares two hypothetical

---

[69]Board of Governors of the Federal Reserve System, *Report to the Congress on Practices of the Consumer Credit Industry in Soliciting and Extending Credit and their Effects on Consumer Debt and Insolvency* (Washington, D.C.: June 2006).

cardholders with identical initial outstanding balances of $2,000 that each make monthly payments of $100. The figure shows how the total amounts of principal are paid down by each of these two cardholders over the course of 12 months, if penalty interest and fees apply. Specifically, cardholder A (1) is assessed a late payment fee in three of those months and (2) has his interest rate increased to a penalty rate of 29 percent after 6 months, while cardholder B does not experience any fees or penalty interest charges. At the end of 12 months, the penalty and fees results in cardholder A paying down $260 or 27 percent less of the total balance owed than does cardholder B who makes on-time payments for the entire period.

Figure 16: Hypothetical Impact of Penalty Interest and Fee Charges on Two Cardholders

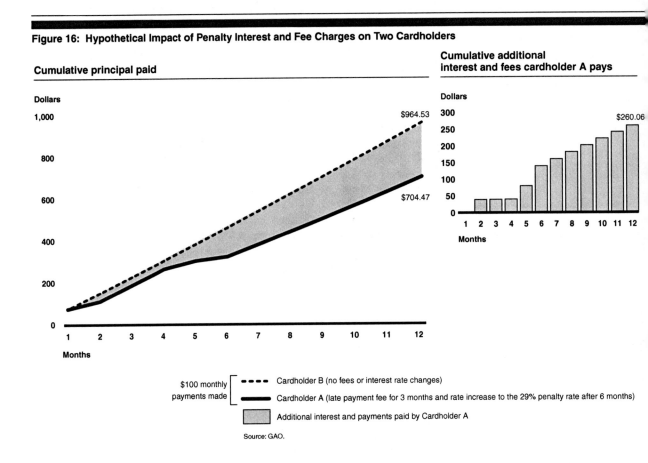

Source: GAO.

| In Some Court Cases, Cardholders Paid Significant Amounts of Penalty Interest and Fees | In reviewing academic literature, hearings, and comment letters to the Federal Reserve, we identified some court cases, including some involving the top six issuers, that indicated that cardholders paid large amounts of penalty interest and fees. For example: |

- In a collections case in Ohio, the $1,963 balance on one cardholder's credit card grew by 183 percent to $5,564 over 6 years, despite the cardholder making few new purchases. According to the court's records, although the cardholder made payments totaling $3,492 over this period, the holder's balance grew as the result of fees and interest charges. According to the court's determinations, between 1997 and 2003, the cardholder was assessed a total of $9,056, including $1,518 in over-limit fees, $1,160 in late fees, $369 in credit insurance, and $6,009 in interest charges and other fees. Although the card issuer had sued to collect, the judge rejected the issuer's collection demand, noting that the cardholder was the victim of unreasonable, unconscionable practices.[70]

- In a June 2004 bankruptcy case filed in the U.S. Bankruptcy Court for the Eastern District of Virginia, the debtor objected to the proofs of claim filed by two companies that had been assigned the debt outstanding on two of the debtor's credit cards. One of the assignees submitted monthly statements for the credit card account it had assumed. The court noted that over a two-year period (during which balance on the account increased from $4,888 to $5,499), the debtor made only $236 in purchases on the account, while making $3,058 in payments, all of which had gone to pay finance charges, late charges, over-limit fees, bad check fees and phone payment fees.[71]

- In a bankruptcy court case filed in July 2003 in North Carolina, 18 debtors filed objections to the claims by one card issuer of the amounts owed on their credit cards.[72] In response to an inquiry by the judge, the card issuer provided data for these accounts that showed that, in the

---

[70]"Comments of the National Consumer Law Center et al. regarding Advance Notice of Proposed Rulemaking Review of the Revolving Credit Rules of Regulation Z," p. 7-9.

[71]*McCarthy vs. eCast Settlement Corporation et al.*, No.04-10493-SSM (Bankr. E.D. Va. filed June 9, 2004).

[72]See *Blair v. Capital One Bank*, No. 02-11400, *Amended Order Overruling Objection to Claim(s)s* (Bankr. W.D. NC filed Feb. 10, 2004) (disposing of, on a consolidated basis, similar objections filed in 18 separate Chapter 13 cases against a common creditor) (Additional docket numbers omitted.).

aggregate, 57 percent of the amounts owed by these 18 accounts at time of their bankruptcy filings represented interest charges and fees. However, the high percentage of interest and fees on these accounts may stem from the size of these principal balances, as some were as low as $95 and none was larger than $1,200.

Regulatory interagency guidance published in 2003 for all depository institutions that issue credit cards may have reduced the potential for cardholders who continue to make minimum payments to experience increasing balances.[73] In this guidance, regulators suggested that card issuers require minimum repayment amounts so that cardholders' current balance would be paid off–amortized–over a reasonable amount of time. In the past, some issuers' minimum monthly payment formulas were such that a full payment may have resulted in little or no principal being paid down, particularly if the cardholder also was assessed any fees during a billing cycle. In such cases, these cardholders' outstanding balances would increase (or negatively amortize). In response to this guidance, some card issuers we interviewed indicated that they have been changing their minimum monthly payment formulas to ensure that credit card balances will be paid off over a reasonable period by including at least some amount of principal in each payment due.

Representatives of card issuers also told us that the regulatory guidance, issued in 2003, addressing credit card workout programs—which allow a distressed cardholder's account to be closed and repaid on a fixed repayment schedule—and other forbearance practices, may help cardholders experiencing financial distress avoid fees. In this guidance, the regulators stated that (1) any workout program offered by an issuer should be designed to have cardholders repay credit card debt within 60 months and (2) to meet this time frame, interest rates and penalty fees may have to be substantially reduced or eliminated so that principal can be repaid. As a result, card issuers are expected to stop imposing penalty fees and interest charges on delinquent card accounts or hardship card accounts enrolled in repayment workout programs. According to this guidance, issuers also can negotiate settlement agreements with cardholders by forgiving a portion of

---

[73]*Credit Card Lending: Account Management and Loss Allowance Guidance* (January 2003), joint guidance issued under the auspices of the Federal Financial Institutions Examination Council by the Office of the Comptroller of the Currency (OCC Bulletin 2003-1), Federal Reserve (Supervisory Letter SR-03-1), Federal Deposit Insurance Corporation (Financial Institution Letter, FIL-2-2003), and Office of Thrift Supervision (OTS Release 03-01).

the amount owed. In exchange, a cardholder can be expected to pay the remaining balance either in a lump-sum payment or by amortizing the balance over a several month period. Staff from OCC and an association of credit counselors told us that, since the issuance of this guidance, they have noticed that card issuers are increasingly both reducing and waiving fees for cardholders who get into financial difficulty. OCC officials also indicated that issuers prefer to facilitate repayment of principal when borrowers adopt debt management plans and tend to reduce or waive fees so the accounts can be amortized. On the other hand, FDIC staff indicated that criteria for waiving fees and penalties are not publicly disclosed to cardholders. These staff noted that most fee waivers occurs after cardholders call and complain to the issuer and are handled on a case-by-case basis.

Data for Some Bankrupt Cardholders Shows Little in Interest and Fees Owed, but Comprehensive Data Were Not Available

Card issuers generally charge-off credit card loans that are no longer collectible because they are in default for either missing a series of payments or filing for bankruptcy. According to the data provided by the six largest issuers, the number of accounts that these issuers collectively had to charge off as a result of the cardholders filing for bankruptcy ranged from about 1.3 million to 1.6 million annually between 2003 and 2005. Collectively, these represented about 1 percent of the six issuers' active accounts during this period. Also, about 60 percent of the accounts were 2 or more months delinquent at the time of the charge-off. Most of the cardholders whose accounts were charged off as the result of a bankruptcy owed small amounts of fees and interest charges at the time of their bankruptcy filing. According to the data the six issuers provided, the average account that they charged off in 2005 owed approximately $6,200 at the time that bankruptcy was filed. Of this amount, the issuers reported that on average 8 percent represented unpaid interest charges; 2 percent unpaid fees, including any unpaid penalty charges; and about 90 percent principal.

However, these data do not provide complete information about the extent to which the financial condition of the cardholders may have been affected by penalty interest and fee charges. First, the amounts that these issuers reported to us as interest and fees due represent only the unpaid amounts that were owed at the time of bankruptcy. According to representatives of the issuers we contacted, each of their firms allocates the amount of any payment received from their customers first to any outstanding interest charges and fees, then allocates any remainder to the principal balance. As a result, the amounts owed at the time of bankruptcy would not reflect any previously paid fees or interest charges. According to representatives of these issuers, data system and recordkeeping limitations prevented them from providing us the amounts of penalty interest and fees assessed on these accounts in the months prior to the bankruptcy filings.

Furthermore, the data do not include information on all of the issuers' cardholders who went bankrupt, but only those whose accounts the issuers charged off as the result of a bankruptcy filing. The issuers also charge off the amounts owed by customers who are delinquent on their payments by more than 180 days, and some of those cardholders may subsequently file for bankruptcy. Such accounts may have accrued larger amounts of unpaid penalty interest and fees than the accounts that were charged off for bankruptcy after being delinquent for less than 180 days, because they would have had more time to be assessed such charges. Representatives of the six issuers told us that they do not maintain records on these customers after they are charged off, and, in many cases, they sell the accounts to collection firms.

Although Penalty Interest and Fees Likely Have Grown as a Share of Credit Card Revenues, Large Card Issuers' Profitability Has Been Stable

Determining the extent to which penalty interest charges and fees contribute to issuers' revenues and profits was difficult because issuers' regulatory filings and other public sources do not include such detail. According to bank regulators, industry analysts, and information reported by the five largest issuers, we estimate that the majority of issuer revenues—around 70 percent in recent years—came from interest charges, and the portion attributable to penalty rates appears to be growing. Of the remaining issuer revenues, penalty fees had increased and were estimated to represent around 10 percent of total issuer revenues. The remainder of issuer revenues came from fees that issuers receive for processing merchants' card transactions and other types of consumer fees. The largest credit card-issuing banks, which are generally the most profitable group of lenders, have not greatly increased their profitability over the last 20 years.

Publicly Disclosed Data on Revenues and Profits from Penalty Interest and Fees Are Limited

Determining the extent to which penalty interest and fee charges are contributing to card issuer revenues and profits is difficult because limited information is available from publicly disclosed financial information. Credit card-issuing banks are subject to various regulations that require them to publicly disclose information about their revenues and expenses. As insured commercial banks, these institutions must file reports of their financial condition, known as call reports, each quarter with their respective federal regulatory agency. In call reports, the banks provide comprehensive balance sheets and income statements disclosing their earnings, including those from their credit card operations. Although the call reports include separate lines for interest income earned, this amount is not further segregated to show, for example, income from the application of penalty interest rates. Similarly, banks report their fee income on the call reports, but this amount includes income from all types of fees, including those related to fiduciary activities, and trading assets and liabilities and is not further segregated to show how much a particular bank has earned from credit card late fees, over-limit fees, or insufficient payment fees.

Another limitation of using call reports to assess the effect of penalty charges on bank revenues is that these reports do not include detailed information on credit card balances that a bank may have sold to other investors through a securitization. As a way of raising additional funds to lend to cardholders, many issuers combine the balances owed on large groups of their accounts and sell these receivables as part of pools of securitized assets to investors. In their call reports, the banks do not report revenue received from cardholders whose balances have been sold into credit card interest and fee income categories.[74] The banks report any gains or losses incurred from the sale of these pooled credit card balances on their call reports as part of noninterest income. Credit card issuing banks generally securitize more than 50 percent of their credit card balances.

Although many card issuers, including most of the top 10 banks, are public companies that must file various publicly available financial disclosures on an ongoing basis with securities regulators, these filings also do not disclose detailed information about penalty interest and fees. We reviewed the public filings by the top five issuers and found that none of the financial statements disaggregated interest income into standard interest and penalty interest charges. In addition, we found that the five banks' public financial statements also had not disaggregated their fee income into penalty fees, service fees, and interchange fees. Instead, most of these card issuers disaggregated their sources of revenue into two broad categories—interest and noninterest income.

---

[74]In accordance with generally accepted accounting principles (Standards of Financial Accounting Statement 140), when card issuers sell any of their credit card receivables as part of a securitization, they subtract the amount of these receivables from the assets shown on their balance sheets.

Majority of Card Issuer Revenues Came from Interest Charges

Although limited information is publicly disclosed, the majority of credit card revenue appears to have come from interest charges. According to regulators, information collected by firms that analyze the credit card industry, and data reported to us by the five of the six largest issuers, the proportion of net interest revenues to card issuers' total revenues is as much as 71 percent. For example, five of the six largest issuers that provided data to us reported that the proportion of their total U.S. card operations income derived from interest charges ranged from 69 to 71 percent between 2003 and 2005.[75]

---

[75]One of the top six largest issuers, Discover, Inc., operates its own transaction processing network; the other issuers process card transactions through the networks operated by Visa International or Mastercard. Because this difference could have reduced the comparability of the data we obtained from these issuers, the information on revenue and profitability aggregated by the third party in response to our data request excludes Discover, Inc.

Figure 17: Example of a Typical Bank's Income Statement

Revenue/expense category	Description
Interest charges ($)/yield (%)	Received from loans to corporate and consumer borrowers, credit card holders carrying balances, etc.
- Cost of funds	Paid on deposits or borrowings from other banks
Net interest income	
+ Noninterest income	From fees or other charges for services paid by borrowers or other customers
Total revenue from operations	
- Credit losses	From the writeoff of amounts of loans or card balances that will not be paid by borrowers who have defaulted
Net risk-adjusted revenue	
- Noninterest expenses	Operating expenses such as postage, utilities, etc., for staff and other noninterest expenses
- Fraud losses	
Noninterest expense + fraud losses	
+ Pre-tax income	
- Taxes	
Net income	

Source: GAO analysis of data reported by the six largest credit card issuers.

We could not precisely determine the extent to which penalty interest charges contribute to this revenue, although the amount of penalty interest that issuers have been assessing has increased. In response to our request, the six largest issuers reported the proportions of their total cardholder accounts that were assessed various rates of interest for 2003 to 2005. On the basis of our analysis of the popular cards issued by these largest issuers, all were charging, on average, default interest rates of around 27 percent. According to the data these issuers provided, the majority of cardholders paid interest rates below 20 percent, but the proportion of their cardholders that paid interest rates at or above 25 percent—which likely represent default rates—has risen from 5 percent in 2003 to 11 percent in 2005. As shown in Figure 18, the proportion of cardholders paying between 15 and 20 percent has also increased, but an issuer representative told us that this likely was due to variable interest rates on cards rising as a result of increases in U.S. market interest rates over the last 3 years.

Figure 18: Proportion of Active Accounts of the Six Largest Card Issuers with Various Interest Rates for Purchases, 2003 to 2005

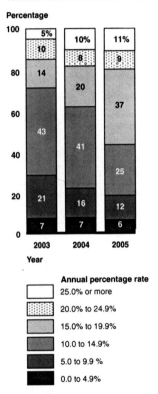

Source: GAO analysis of data reported by the six largest credit card issuers.

Although we could not determine the amounts of penalty interest the card issuers received, the increasing proportion of accounts assessed rates of 25 percent suggests a significant increase in interest revenues. For example, a cardholder carrying a stable balance of $1,000 and paying 10 percent interest would pay approximately $100 annually, while a cardholder carrying the same stable balance but paying 25 percent would pay $250 to the card issuer annually. Although we did not obtain any information on the size of balances owed by the cardholders of the largest issuers, the proportion of the revenues these issuers received from cardholders paying penalty interest rates may also be greater than 11 percent because such cardholders may have balances larger than the $2,500 average for 2005 that the issuers reported to us.

Fees Represented the Remainder of Issuer Revenues

The remaining card issuer revenues largely come from noninterest sources, including merchant and consumer fees. Among these are penalty fees and other consumer fees, as well as fees that issuers receive as part of processing card transactions for merchants.

Penalty Fees Had Increased

Although no comprehensive data exist publicly, various sources we identified indicated that penalty fees represent around 10 percent of issuers' total revenues and had generally increased. We identified various sources that gave estimates of penalty fee income as a percentage of card issuers' total revenues that ranged from 9 to 13 percent:

- Analysis of the data the top six issuers provided to us indicated that each of these issuers assessed an average of about $1.2 billion in penalty fees for cardholders that made late payments or exceeded their credit limit in 2005. In total, these six issuers reported assessing $7.4 billion for these two penalty fees that year, about 12 percent of the $60.3 billion in total interest and consumer fees (penalty fees and fees for other cardholder services).[76]

- According to a private firm that assists credit card banks with buying and selling portfolios of credit card balance receivables, penalty fees likely represented about 13 percent of total card issuer revenues. According to an official with this firm, it calculated this estimate by using information from 15 of the top 20 issuers, as well as many smaller banks, that together represent up to 80 percent of the total credit card industry.[77]

---

[76]We were not provided information on the portion of revenues these issuers earned from these penalty fees and consumer fees.

[77]Although we were not able to completely assess the reliability of this organization's data and its methods for making its estimates of industry revenue components, we present this information because it appeared to be similar to the proportions reported by the top six issuers that provided us data.

- An estimate from an industry research firm that publishes data on credit card issuer activities indicated that penalty fees represented about 9 percent of issuer total revenues.

Issuers Also Collect Revenues from Processing Merchant Card Transactions

When a consumer makes a purchase with a credit card, the merchant selling the goods does not receive the full purchase price. When the cardholder presents the credit card to make a purchase, the merchant transmits the cardholder's account number and the amount of the transaction to the merchant's bank.[78] The merchant's bank forwards this information to the card association, such as Visa or Mastercard, requesting authorization for the transaction. The card association forwards the authorization request to the bank that issued the card to the cardholder. The issuing bank then responds with its authorization or denial to the merchant's bank and then to the merchant. After the transaction is approved, the issuing bank will send the purchase amount, less an interchange fee, to the merchant's bank. The interchange fee is established by the card association. Before crediting the merchant's account, the merchant's bank will subtract a servicing fee. These transaction fees— called interchange fees—are commonly about 2 percent of the total purchase price. As shown in figure 19, the issuing banks generally earn about $2.00 for every $100 purchased as interchange fee revenue. In addition, the card association receives a transaction processing fee. The card associations, such as Visa or Mastercard, assess the amount of these fees and also conduct other important activities, including imposing rules for issuing cards, authorizing, clearing and settling transactions, advertising and promoting the network brand, and allocating revenues among the merchants, merchant's bank, and card issuer.

---

[78]The bank that a merchant uses to process its credit card transactions is known as the acquiring bank.

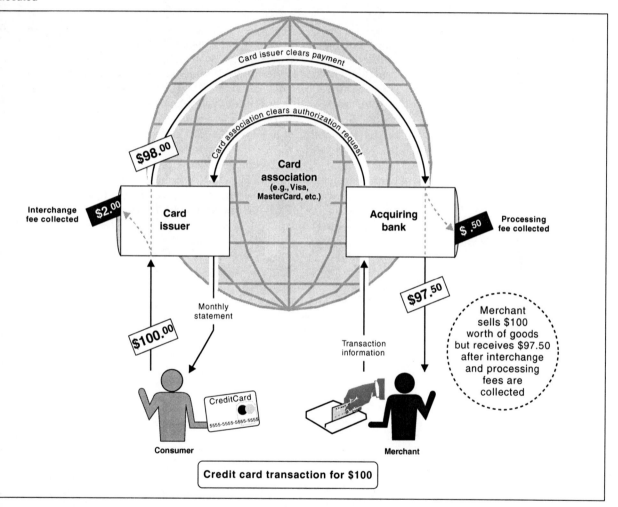

Sources: GAO (analysis); Art Explosion (images).

In addition to penalty fees and interchange fees, the remaining noninterest revenues for card issuers include other consumer fees or other fees. Card issuers collect annual fees, cash advance fees, balance transfer fees, and other fees from their cardholders. In addition, card issuers collect other revenues, such as from credit insurance. According to estimates by industry analyst firms, such revenues likely represented about 8 to 9 percent of total issuer revenues.

Large Credit Card Issuer Profitability Has Been Stable

The profits of credit card-issuing banks, which are generally the most profitable group of lenders, have been stable over the last 7 years. A commonly used indicator of profitability is the return on assets ratio (ROA). This ratio, which is calculated by dividing a company's income by its total assets, shows how effectively a business uses its assets to generate profits. In annual reports to Congress, the Federal Reserve provides data on the profitability of larger credit card issuers—which included 17 banks in 2004.[79] Figure 20 shows the average ROA using pretax income for these large credit card issuers compared with pretax ROA of all commercial banks during the period 1986 to 2004. In general, the large credit card issuers earned an average return of 3.12 percent over this period, which was more than twice as much as the 1.49 percent average returns earned by all commercial banks.

---

[79]See Federal Reserve System, *Profitability of Credit Card Operations*, June 2005. The data included in these reports are for all commercial banks with at least $200 million in yearly average assets (loans to individuals plus securitizations) and at least 50 percent of assets in consumer lending, of which 90 percent must be in the form of revolving credit.

Figure 20: Average Pretax Return on Assets for Large Credit Card Banks and All Commercial Banks, 1986 to 2004

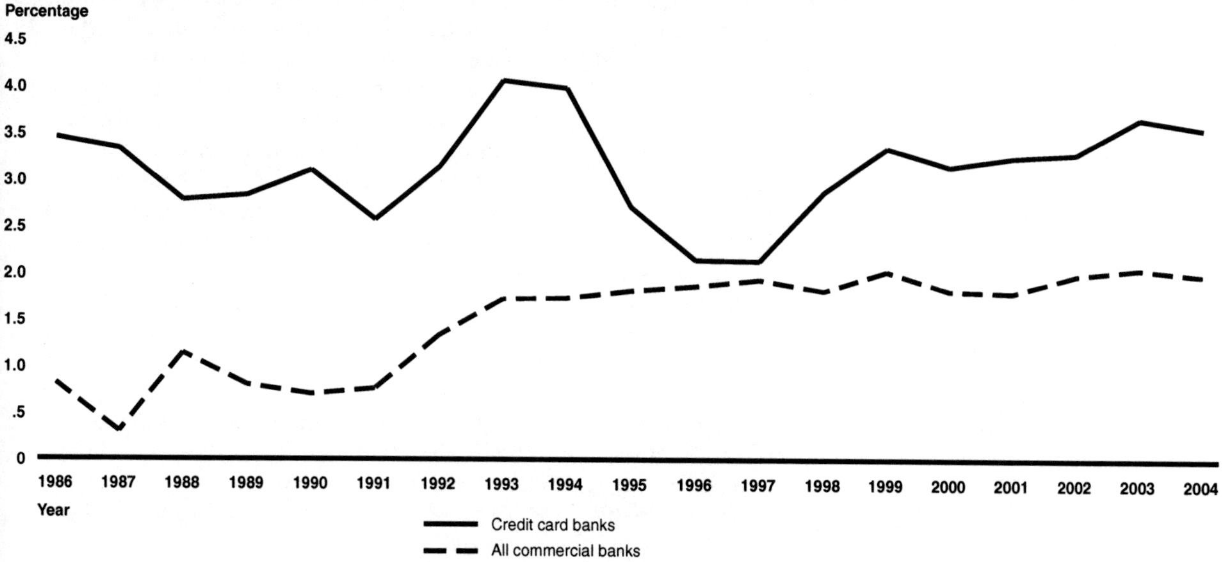

Percentage

Credit card banks
All commercial banks

Source: Federal Reserve Board.

As shown in the figure above, the ROA for larger credit card banks, although fluctuating more widely during the 1990s, has generally been stable since 1999, with returns in the 3.0 to 3.5 percent range. The return on assets for the large card issuers peaked in 1993 at 4.1 percent and has declined to 3.55 percent in 2004. In contrast, the profitability of all commercial banks has been generally increasing over this period, rising more than 140 percent between 1986 and 2004. Similar to the data for all larger credit card issuers, data that five of the six largest issuers provided to us indicated that their profitability also has been stable in the 3 years between 2003 and 2005. These five issuers reported that the return on their pretax earnings over their credit card balances over this 3-year period ranged from about 3.6 percent to 4.1 percent.

Because of the high interest rates that issuers charge and variable rate pricing, credit card lending generally is the most profitable type of consumer lending, despite the higher rate of loan losses that issuers incur on cards. Rates charged on credit cards generally are the highest of any consumer lending category because they are extensions of credit that are not secured by any collateral from the borrower. In contrast, other common types of consumer lending, such as automobile loans or home mortgages, involve the extension of a fixed amount of credit under fixed terms of repayment that are secured by the underlying asset—the car or the house—which the lender can repossess in the event of nonpayment by the borrower. Collateral and fixed repayment terms reduce the risk of loss to the lender, enabling them to charge lower interest rates on such loans. In contrast, credit card loans, which are unsecured, available to large and heterogeneous populations, and repayable on flexible terms at the cardholders' convenience, present greater risks and have commensurately higher interest rates. For example, according to Federal Reserve statistics, the interest rate charged on cards by lenders generally has averaged above 16 percent since 1980, while the average rate charged on car loans since then has averaged around 10 percent. Borrowers may be more likely to cease making payments on their credit cards if they become financially distressed than they would on other loans that are secured by an asset they could lose. For example, the percentage of credit card loans that banks have had to charge off averaged above 4 percent between 2003 and 2005; in contrast, charge-offs for other types of consumer loans average about 2 percent, with charge-offs for mortgage loans averaging less than 1 percent, during those 3 years. (App. III provides additional detail about the factors that affect the profitability of credit card issuers.)

Conclusions

Credit cards provide various benefits to their cardholders, including serving as a convenient way to pay for goods and services and providing additional funds at rates of interest generally lower than those consumers would have paid to borrow on cards in the past. However, the penalties for late payments or other behaviors involving card use have risen significantly in recent years. Card issuers note that their use of risk-based pricing structures with multiple interest rates and fees has allowed them to offer credit cards to cardholders at costs that are commensurate with the risks presented by different types of customers, including those who previously might not have been able to obtain credit cards. On the whole, a large number of cardholders experience greater benefits—either by using their cards for transactions without incurring any direct expense or by enjoying generally lower costs for borrowing than prevailed in the past—from using credit cards than was previously possible, but the habits or financial circumstances of other cardholders also could result in these consumers facing greater costs than they did in the past.

The expansion and increased complexity of card rates, fees, and issuer practices has heightened the need for consumers to receive clear disclosures that allow them to more easily understand the costs of using cards. In the absence of any regulatory or legal limits on the interest or fees that cards can impose, providing consumers with adequate information on credit card costs and practices is critical to ensuring that vigorous competition among card issuers produces a market that provides the best possible rates and terms for U.S. consumers. Our work indicates that the disclosure materials that the largest card issuers typically provided under the existing regulations governing credit cards had many serious weaknesses that reduced their usefulness to the consumers they are intended to help. Although these regulations likely were adequate when card rates and terms were less complex, the disclosure materials they produce for cards today, which have a multitude of terms and conditions that can affect cardholders' costs, have proven difficult for consumers to use in finding and understanding important information about their cards. Although providing some key information, current disclosures also give prominence to terms, such as minimum finance charge or balance computation method, that are less significant to consumers' costs and do not adequately emphasize terms such as those cardholder actions that could cause their card issuer to raise their interest rate to a high default rate. Because part of the reason that current disclosure materials may be less effective is that they were designed in an era when card rates and terms were less complex, the Federal Reserve also faces the challenge of creating disclosure requirements that are more flexible to allow them to be adjusted more quickly as new card features are introduced and others become less common.

The Federal Reserve, which has adopted these regulations, has recognized these problems, and its current review of the open-end credit rules of Regulation Z presents an opportunity to improve the disclosures applicable to credit cards. Based on our work, we believe that disclosures that are simpler, better organized, and use designs and formats that comply with best practices and industry standards for readability and usability would be more effective. Our work and the experiences of other regulators also confirmed that involving experts in readability and testing documents with actual consumers can further improve any resulting disclosures. The Federal Reserve has indicated that it has begun to involve consumers in the design of new model disclosures, but it has not completed these efforts to date, and new model disclosures are not expected to be issued until 2007 or 2008. Federal Reserve staff noted that they recognize the challenge of how best to incorporate the variety of information that consumers may need to understand the costs of their cards in clear and concise disclosure materials. Until such efforts are complete, consumers will continue to face difficulties in using disclosure materials to better understand and compare costs of credit cards. In addition, until more understandable disclosures are issued, the ability of well-informed consumers to spur additional competition among issuers in credit card pricing is hampered.

Definitively determining the extent to which credit card penalty interest and fees contribute to personal bankruptcies and the profits and revenues of card issuers is difficult given the lack of comprehensive, publicly available data. Penalty interest and fees can contribute to the total debt owed by cardholders and decrease the funds that a cardholder could have used to reduce debt and possibly avoid bankruptcy. However, many consumers file for bankruptcy as the result of significant negative life events, such as divorces, job losses, or health problems, and the role that credit cards play in avoiding or accelerating such filings is not known. Similarly, the limited available information on card issuer operations indicates that penalty fees and interest are a small but growing part of such firms' revenues. With the profitability of the largest card issuers generally being stable over recent years, the increased revenues gained from penalty interest and fees may be offsetting the generally lower amounts of interest that card issuers collect from the majority of their cardholders. These results appear to indicate that while most cardholders likely are better off, a smaller number of cardholders paying penalty interest and fees are accounting for more of issuer revenues than they did in the past. This further emphasizes the importance of taking steps to ensure that all cardholders receive disclosures that help them clearly understand their card costs and how their own behavior can affect those costs.

Recommendation for Executive Action

As part of its effort to increase the effectiveness of disclosure materials used to inform consumers of rates, fees, and other terms that affect the costs of using credit cards, the Chairman, Federal Reserve should ensure that such disclosures, including model forms and formatting requirements, more clearly emphasize those terms that can significantly affect cardholder costs, such as the actions that can cause default or other penalty pricing rates to be imposed.

Agency Comments and Our Evaluation

We provided a draft of this report to the Federal Reserve, OCC, FDIC, the Federal Trade Commission, the National Credit Union Administration, and the Office of Thrift Supervision for their review and comment. In a letter from the Federal Reserve, the Director of the Division of Consumer and

Community Affairs agreed with the findings of our report that credit card pricing has become more complex and that the disclosures required under Regulation Z could be improved with the input of consumers. To this end, the Director stated that the Board is conducting extensive consumer testing to identify the most important information to consumers and how disclosures can be simplified to reduce current complexity. Using this information, the Director said that the Board would develop new model disclosure forms with the assistance of design consultants. If appropriate, the Director said the Board may develop suggestions for statutory changes for congressional consideration.

We also received technical comments from the Federal Reserve and OCC, which we have incorporated in this report as appropriate. FDIC, the Federal Trade Commission, the National Credit Union Administration, and the Office of Thrift Supervision did not provide comments.

As agreed with your offices, unless you publicly announce its contents earlier, we plan no further distribution of this report until 30 days after the date of this report. At that time, we will send copies of this report to the Chairman, Permanent Subcommittee on Investigations, Senate Committee on Homeland Security and Governmental Affairs; the Chairman, FDIC; the Chairman, Federal Reserve; the Chairman, Federal Trade Commission; the Chairman, National Credit Union Administration; the Comptroller of the Currency; and the Director, Office of Thrift Supervision and to interested congressional committees. We will also make copies available to others upon request. The report will be available at no charge on the GAO Web site at http://www.gao.gov.

If you or your staff have any questions regarding this report, please contact me at (202) 512-8678 or woodd@gao.gov. Contact points for our Offices of Congressional Relations and Public Affairs may be found on the last page of this report. Key contributors to this report are listed in appendix IV.

Sincerely yours,

David G. Wood

David G. Wood
Director, Financial Markets
and Community Investment

Objectives, Scope and Methodology

Our objectives were to determine (1) how the interest, fees, and other practices that affect the pricing structure of cards from the largest U.S. issuers have evolved, and cardholders' experiences under these pricing structures in recent years; (2) how effectively the issuers disclose the pricing structures of cards to their cardholders; (3) whether credit card debt and penalty interest and fees contribute to cardholder bankruptcies; and (4) the extent to which penalty interest and fees contribute to the revenues and profitability of issuers' credit card operations.

Methodology for Identifying the Evolution of Pricing Structures

To identify how the pricing structure of cards from the largest U.S. issuers has evolved, we analyzed disclosure documents from 2003 to 2005 for 28 popular cards that were issued by the six largest U.S. card issuers, as measured by total outstanding receivables as of December 31, 2004 (see fig. 2 in the body of this report). These issuers were Bank of America; Capital One Bank; Chase Bank USA, N.A.; Citibank (South Dakota), N.A.; Discover Financial Services; and MBNA America Bank, N.A. Representatives for these six issuers identified up to five of their most popular cards and provided us actual disclosure materials, including cardmember agreements and direct mail applications and solicitations used for opening an account for each card. We calculated descriptive statistics for various interest rates and fees and the frequency with which cards featured other practices, such as methods for calculating finance charges. We determined that these cards likely represented the pricing and terms that applied to the majority of U.S. cardholders because the top six issuers held almost 80 percent of consumer credit card debt and as much as 61 percent of total U.S. credit card accounts.

We did not include in our analysis of popular cards any cards offered by credit card issuers that engage primarily in subprime lending. Subprime lending generally refers to extending credit to borrowers who exhibit characteristics indicating a significantly higher risk of default than traditional bank lending customers. Such issuers could have pricing structures and other terms significantly different to those of the popular cards offered by the top issuers. As a result, our analysis may underestimate the range of interest rate and fee levels charged on the entire universe of cards. To identify historical rate and fee levels, we primarily evaluated the Federal Reserve Board's G.19 Consumer Credit statistical release for 1972 to 2005 and a paper written by a Federal Reserve Bank staff, which included more than 150 cardmember agreements from 15 of the largest U.S. issuers in 1997 to 2002.[1]

To evaluate cardholders' experiences with credit card pricing structures in recent years, we obtained proprietary data on the extent to which issuers assessed various interest rate levels and fees for active accounts from the six largest U.S. issuers listed above for 2003, 2004, and 2005. We obtained data directly from issuers because no comprehensive sources existed to show the extent to which U.S. cardholders were paying penalty interest rates. Combined, these issuers reported more than 180 million active accounts, or about 60 percent of total active accounts reported by CardWeb.com, Inc. These accounts also represented almost $900 billion in credit card purchases in 2005, according to these issuers. To preserve the anonymity of the data, these issuers engaged legal counsel at the law firm Latham & Watkins, LLP, to which they provided their data on interest rate and fee assessments, which then engaged Argus Information and Advisory Services, LLC, a third-party analytics firm, to aggregate the data, and then supplied it to us. Although we originally provided a more comprehensive data request to these issuers, we agreed to a more limited request with issuer representatives as a result of these firms' data availability and processing limitations. We discussed steps that were taken to attempt to ensure that the data provided to us were complete and accurate with representatives of these issuers and the third party analytics firm. We also shared a draft of this report with the supervisory agencies of these issuers. However, we did not have access to the issuers' data systems to fully assess the reliability of the data or the systems that housed them. Therefore, we present these data in our report only as representations made to us by the six largest issuers.

Methodology for Assessing Effectiveness of Disclosures

To determine how effectively card issuers disclose to cardholders the rates, fees, and other terms related to their credit cards, we contracted with UserWorks, Inc., a private usability consulting firm, which conducted three separate evaluations of a sample of disclosure materials. We provided the usability consultant with a cardmember agreement and solicitation letter for one card from four representative credit card issuers—a total of four cards and eight disclosure documents. The first evaluation, a readability assessment, used computer-facilitated formulas to predict the grade level

---

[1]M. Furletti, "Credit Card Pricing Developments and Their Disclosure," Federal Reserve Bank of Philadelphia's Payment Cards Center, January 2003.

required to understand the materials. Readability formulas measure the elements of writing that can be subjected to mathematical calculation, such as average number of syllables in words or numbers of words in sentences in the text. The consultant applied the following industry-standard formulas to the documents: Flesch Grade Level, Frequency of Gobbledygook (FOG), and the Simplified Measure of Gobbledygook (SMOG). Using these formulas, the consultant measured the grade levels at which the disclosure documents were written overall, as well as for selected sections. Secondly, the usability consultant conducted an heuristic evaluation that assessed how well these card disclosure documents adhered to a recognized set of principles or industry best practices. In the absence of best practices specifically applicable to credit card disclosures, the consultant used guidelines from the U.S. Securities and Exchange Commission's 1998 guidebook *Plain English Handbook: How to Create Clear SEC Disclosure Documents.*

Finally, the usability consultant tested how well actual consumers were able to use the documents to identify and understand information about card fees and other practices and used the results to identify problem areas. The consultant conducted these tests with 12 consumers.[2] To ensure sample diversity, the participants were selected to represent the demographics of the U.S. adult population in terms of education, income, and age. While the materials used for the readability and usability assessments appeared to be typical of the large issuers' disclosures, the results cannot be generalized to materials that were not reviewed.

To obtain additional information on consumers' level of awareness and understanding of their key credit card terms, we also conducted in-depth, structured interviews in December 2005 with a total of 112 adult cardholders in three locations: Boston, Chicago, and San Francisco.[3] We contracted with OneWorld Communications, Inc., a market research organization, to recruit a sample of cardholders that generally resembled the demographic makeup of the U.S. population in terms of age, education levels, and income. However, the cardholders recruited for the interviews did not form a random, statistically representative sample of the U.S.

---

[2]According to the consultant, testing with small numbers of individuals can generally identify many of the problems that can affect the readability and usability of materials.

[3]We conducted these interviews when preparing our report on the feasibility and usefulness of requiring additional disclosures to cardholders on the consequences of making only the minimum payment on their cards.

population and therefore cannot be generalized to the population of all U.S. cardholders. Cardholders had to speak English, have owned at least one general-purpose credit card for a minimum of 12 months, and have not participated in more than one focus group or similar in-person study in the 12 months prior to the interview. We gathered information about the cardholders' knowledge of credit card terms and conditions, and assessed cardholders' use of card disclosure materials by asking them a number of open- and closed-ended questions.

Methodology for Determining How Penalty Charges Contribute to Bankruptcy

To determine whether credit card debt and penalty interest and fees contribute to cardholder bankruptcies, we interviewed Department of Justice staff responsible for overseeing bankruptcy courts and trustees about the availability of data on credit card penalty charges in materials submitted by consumers or issuers as part of bankruptcy filings or collections cases. We also interviewed two attorneys that assist consumers with bankruptcy filings. In addition, we reviewed studies that analyzed credit card and bankruptcy issues published by various academic researchers, the Congressional Research Service, and the Congressional Budget Office. We did not attempt to assess the reliability of all of these studies to the same, full extent. However, because of the prominence of some of these data sources, and frequency of use of this data by other researchers, as well as the fact that much of the evidence is corroborated by other evidence, we determined that citing these studies was appropriate.

We also analyzed aggregated card account data provided by the six largest issuers (as previously discussed) to measure the amount of credit card interest charges and fees owed at the time these accounts were charged off as a result of becoming subject to bankruptcy filing. We also spoke with representatives of the largest U.S. credit card issuers, as well as representatives of consumer groups and industry associations, and with academic researchers that conduct analysis on the credit card industry.

Methodology for Determining How Penalty Charges Contribute to Issuer Revenues

To determine the extent to which penalty interest and fees contributed to the revenues and profitability of issuers' credit card operations, we reviewed the extent to which penalty charges are disclosed in bank regulatory reports—the call reports—and in public disclosures—such as annual reports (10-Ks) and quarterly reports (10-Qs) made by publicly traded card issuers. We analyzed data reported by the Federal Reserve on the profitability of commercial bank card issuers with at least $200 million in yearly average assets (loans to individuals plus securitizations) and at least 50 percent of assets in consumer lending, of which 90 percent must be in the form of revolving credit. In 2004, the Federal Reserve reported that 17 banks had card operations with at least this level of activity in 2004. We also analyzed information from the Federal Deposit Insurance Corporation, which analyzes data for all federally insured banks and savings institutions and publishes aggregated data on those with various lending activity concentrations, including a group of 33 banks that, as of December 2005, had credit card operations that exceeded 50 percent of their total assets and securitized receivables.

We also analyzed data reported to us by the six largest card issuers on their revenues and profitability of their credit card operations for 2003, 2004, and 2005. We also reviewed data on revenues compiled by industry analysis firms, including *Card Industry Directory* published by Sourcemedia, and R.K. Hammer. Because of the proprietary nature of their data, representatives for Sourcemedia and R.K. Hammer were not able to provide us with information sufficient for us to assess the reliability of their data. However, we analyzed and presented some information from these sources because we were able to corroborate their information with each other and with data from sources of known reliability, such as regulatory data, and we attribute their data to them.

We also interviewed broker-dealer financial analysts who monitor activities by credit card issuers to identify the extent to which various sources of income contribute to card issuers' revenues and profitability. We attempted to obtain the latest in a series of studies of card issuer profitability that Visa, Inc. traditionally has compiled. However, staff from this organization said that this report is no longer being made publicly available.

We discussed issues relevant to this report with various organizations, including representatives of 13 U.S. credit card issuers and card networks, 2 trade associations, 4 academics, 4 federal bank agencies, 4 national consumer interest groups, 2 broker dealer analysts that study credit card issuers for large investors, and a commercial credit-rating agency. We also obtained technical comments on a draft of this report from representatives of the issuers that supplied data for this study.

Consumer Bankruptcies Have Risen Along with Debt

Consumer bankruptcies have increased significantly over the past 25 years. As shown in figure 21 below, consumer bankruptcy filings rose from about 287,000 in 1980 to more than 2 million as of December 31, 2005, about a 609 percent increase over the last 25 years.[1]

Figure 21: U.S. Consumer Bankruptcy Filings, 1980-2005

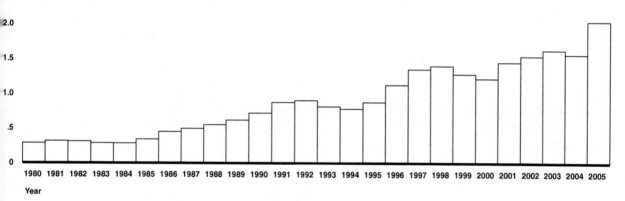

Consumer filings (in millions)

Year

Source: GAO analysis of Congressional Research Service report and Administrative Office of the United States Courts data.

Debt Levels Have Also Risen

The expansion of consumers' overall indebtedness is one of the explanations cited for the significant increase in bankruptcy filings. As shown in figure 22, consumers' use of debt has expanded over the last 25 years, increasing more than 720 percent from about $1.4 trillion in 1980 to about $11.5 trillion in 2005.

---

[1]Of the filings in 2005, approximately 80 percent were Chapter 7 cases and the other 20 percent were Chapter 13 cases.

Figure 22: U.S. Household Debt, 1980-2005

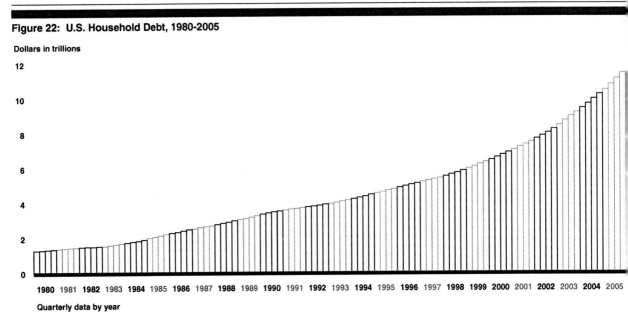

Dollars in trillions

Quarterly data by year

Source: Board of Governors of the Federal Reserve System.

Some researchers have been commenting on the rise in overall indebtedness as a contributor to the rise in bankruptcies for some time. For example, in a 1997 congressional testimony, a Congressional Budget Office official noted that the increase in consumer bankruptcy filings and the increase in household indebtedness appeared to be correlated.[2] Also, an academic paper that summarized existing literature on bankruptcy found that some consumer bankruptcies were either directly or indirectly caused by heavy consumer indebtedness, specifically pointing to the high correlation between consumer bankruptcies and consumer debt-to-income ratios.[3]

[2]Kim Kowalewski, "Consumer Debt and Bankruptcy," Congressional Budget Office testimony before the United States Senate Subcommittee on Administrative Oversight and the Courts, Committee on the Judiciary, 105th Congress, 1st sess., Apr. 11, 1997.

[3]Todd J. Zywicki, "An Economic Analysis of the Consumer Bankruptcy Crisis," *Northwestern University Law Review*, 99, no.4, (2005).

Beyond total debt, some researchers and others argue that the rise in bankruptcies also was related to the rise in credit debt, in particular. As shown in figure 23, the amount of credit card debt reported also has risen from $237 billion to about $802 billion—a 238 percent increase between 1990 and 2005.[4]

---

[4]In addition to capturing amounts outstanding on credit cards, the number reported in the Federal Reserve's survey of consumer debt for revolving debt also includes other types of revolving debt. However, Congressional Research Service staff familiar with the survey's results indicated that the vast majority of the amount reported as revolving debt is from credit cards.

Figure 23: Credit Card and Other Revolving and Nonrevolving Debt Outstanding, 1990 to 2005

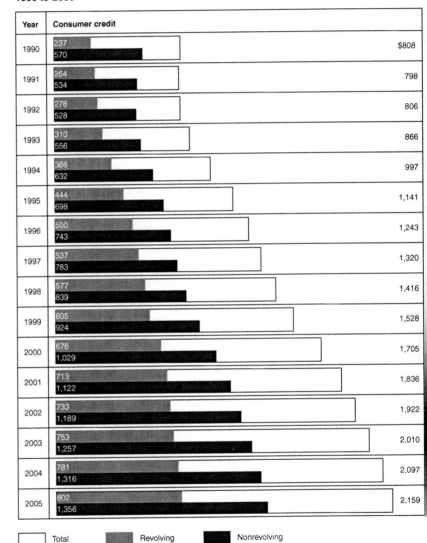

Year	Consumer credit		
1990	237 / 570		$808
1991	264 / 534		798
1992	278 / 528		806
1993	310 / 556		866
1994	366 / 632		997
1995	444 / 698		1,141
1996	500 / 743		1,243
1997	537 / 783		1,320
1998	577 / 839		1,416
1999	605 / 924		1,528
2000	676 / 1,029		1,705
2001	713 / 1,122		1,836
2002	733 / 1,189		1,922
2003	753 / 1,257		2,010
2004	781 / 1,316		2,097
2005	802 / 1,356		2,159

Total Revolving Nonrevolving

Source: GAO analysis of Congressional Research Service report data.

Increased Access to Credit Cards by Lower-income Households Raised Concerns

Rather than total credit card debt alone, some researchers argued that growth in credit card use and indebtedness by lower-income households has contributed to the rise in bankruptcies. In the survey of consumer finances conducted every 3 years, the Federal Reserve reports on the use and indebtedness on credit cards by households overall and also by income percentiles. As shown in figure 24 below, the latest Federal Reserve survey results indicated the greatest increase of families reporting credit card debt occurred among those in the lowest 20 percent of household income between 1998 and 2001.

Figure 24: Percent of Households Holding Credit Card Debt by Household Income, 1998, 2001, and 2004

Percentile of income	1998	2001	2004
Less than 20	24.5	30.3	28.8
20-39.9	40.9	44.5	42.9
40-59.9	50.1	52.8	55.1
60-79.9	57.4	52.6	56.0
80-89.9	53.1	50.3	57.6
90-100	42.1	33.1	38.5
All	44.1	44.4	46.2

Source: Federal Reserve Board's Survey of Consumer Finances.

In the last 15 years, credit card companies have greatly expanded the marketing of credit cards, including to households with lower incomes than previously had been offered cards. An effort by credit card issuers to expand its customer base in an increasingly competitive market dramatically increased credit card solicitations. According to one study, more than half of credit cards held by consumers are the result of receiving mail solicitations.[5] According to another academic research paper, credit card issuers have increased the number of mail solicitations they send to consumers by more than five times since 1990, from 1.1 billion to 5.23 billion in 2004, or a little over 47 solicitations per household. The research paper also found that wealthier families receive the highest number of solicitations but that low-income families were more likely to open them.[6] As shown in figure 25 above, the Federal Reserve's survey results indicated that the number of lower income households with credit cards has also grown the most during 1998 to 2001, reflecting issuers' willingness to grant greater access to credit cards to such households than in the past.

Levels of Financial Distress Have Remained Stable among Households

The ability of households to make the payments on their debt appeared to be keeping pace with their incomes as their total household debt burden levels—which measure their payments required on their debts as percentage of household incomes—have remained relatively constant since the 1980s. As shown below in figure 25, Federal Reserve statistics show that the aggregate debt burden ratio for U.S. households has generally fluctuated between 10.77 percent to 13.89 percent between 1990 to 2005, which are similar to the levels for this ratio that were observed during the 1980s. Also shown in figure 25 are the Federal Reserve's statistics on the household financial obligations ratio, which compares the total payments that a household must make for mortgages, consumer debt, auto leases, rent, homeowners insurance, and real estate taxes to its after-tax income. Although this ratio has risen from around 16 percent in 1980 to over 18 percent in 2005—representing an approximately 13 percent increase—Federal Reserve staff researchers indicated that it does not necessarily indicate an increase in household financial stress because

---

[5]Vertis, "*Financial Direct Mail Readers Interested in Credit Card Offers,*" (Jan. 25, 2005), cited in the Consumer Federation of America testimony before the Committee on Banking, Housing, and Urban Affairs of the United States Senate, "*Examining the Current Legal and Regulatory Requirements and Industry Practices for Credit Card Issuers with Respect to Consumer Disclosures and Marketing Efforts,*" 109th Congress, 2nd sess., May, 17, 2005.

[6]Amdetsion Kidane and Sandip Mukerji, "Characteristics of Consumers Targeted and Neglected by Credit Card Companies," *Financial Services Review*, 13, no. 3, (2004), cited in the Consumer Federation of America testimony before the Committee on Banking, Housing and Urban Affairs of the United States Senate, "*Examining the Current Legal and Regulatory Requirements and Industry Practices for Credit Card Issuers with Respect to Consumer Disclosures and Marketing Efforts,*" 109th Congress, 2nd sess., May, 17, 2005.

much of this increase appeared to be the result of increased use of credit cards for transactions and more households with cards.[7]

Figure 25: U.S. Household Debt Burden and Financial Obligations Ratios, 1980 to 2005

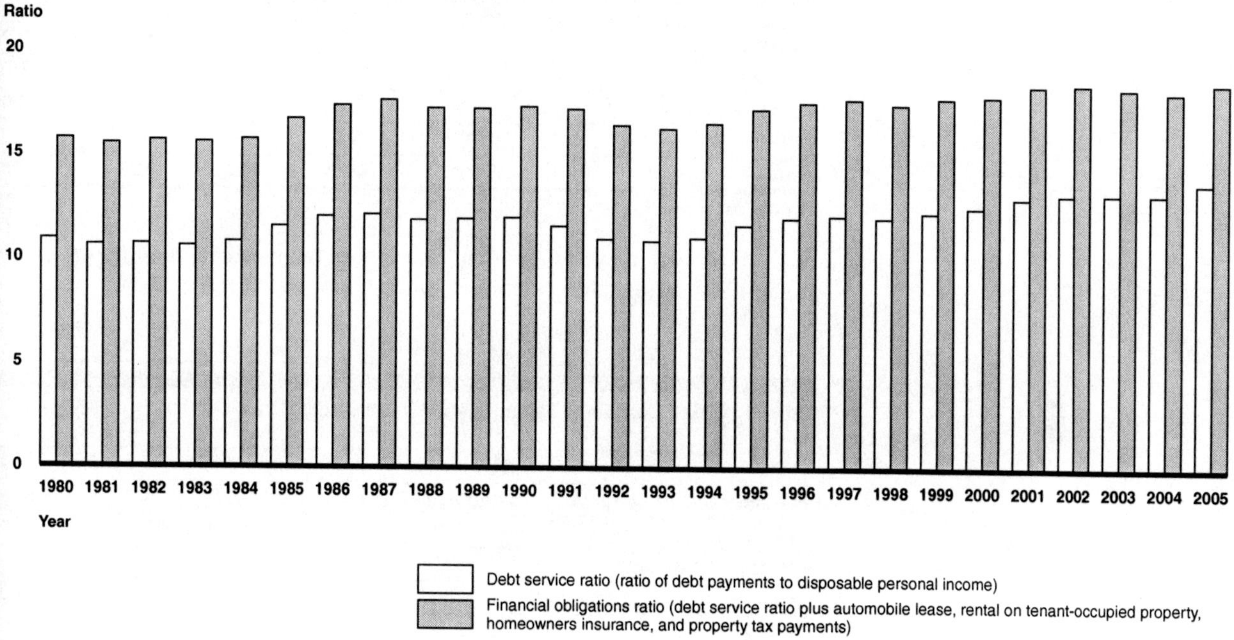
Ratio
20
15
10
5
0
1980 1981 1982 1983 1984 1985 1986 1987 1988 1989 1990 1991 1992 1993 1994 1995 1996 1997 1998 1999 2000 2001 2002 2003 2004 2005
Year
Debt service ratio (ratio of debt payments to disposable personal income)
Financial obligations ratio (debt service ratio plus automobile lease, rental on tenant-occupied property, homeowners insurance, and property tax payments)

Source: Federal Reserve.

In addition, credit card debt remains a small portion of overall household debt, including those with the lowest income levels. As shown in table 2, credit card balances as a percentage of total household debt actually have been declining since the 1990s.

[7]Board of Governors of the Federal Reserve System, *Report to the Congress on Practices of the Consumer Credit Industry in Soliciting and Extending Credit and their Effects on Consumer Debt and Insolvency* (Washington, D.C.: June 2006).

Table 2: Portion of Credit Card Debt Held by Households

Type of debt	1995	1998	2001	2004
Amount of debt of all families, distributed by type of debt				
Secured home loan	80.7	78.9	81.4	83.7
Lines of credit not secured by residential property	0.6	0.3	0.5	0.7
Installment loans	12.0	13.1	12.3	11.0
Credit card balances	3.9	3.9	3.4	3.0
Other	2.9	3.7	2.3	1.6
Total	**100**	**100**	**100**	**100**

Source: Federal Reserve.

Also, as shown in table 3, median credit card balances for the lowest-income households has remained stable from 1998 through 2004.

Table 3: Credit Card Debt Balances Held by Household Income[8]

	1998	2001	2004
Median value of holdings for families holding credit card debt			
All families	$1,900	$2,000	$2,200
Percentile of income			
Less than 20	$1,000	$1,100	$1,000
20-39.9	$1,300	$1,300	$1,900
40-59.9	$2,100	$2,100	$2,200
60-79.9	$2,400	$2,400	$3,000
80-89.9	$2,200	$4,000	$2,700
90-100	$3,300	$3,000	$4,000

Source: Federal Reserve.

As shown in figure 26 below, the number of households in the twentieth percentile of income or less that reportedly were in financial distress has remained relatively stable.

---

[8]The 1998 median credit card balance in 2001 dollars; 2001 and 2004 median credit card balances in 2004 dollars.

Figure 26: Households Reporting Financial Distress by Household Income, 1995 through 2004

Percentile of income	1995	1998	2001	2004
All	11.7	13.6	11.8	12.2
Less than 20	27.5	29.9	29.3	27.0
20-39.9	18.0	18.3	16.6	18.6
40-59.9	9.9	15.8	12.3	13.7
60-79.9	7.7	9.8	6.5	7.10
80-89.9	4.7	3.5	3.5	2.4
90-100	2.3	2.8	2.0	1.8

Source: Federal Reserve Survey of Consumer Finances.

As shown in figure 26 above, more lower-income households generally reported being in financial distress than did other households in most of the other higher-income groups. In addition, the lowest-income households in the aggregate generally did not exhibit greater levels of distress over the last 20 years, as the proportion of households that reported distress was higher in the 1990s than in 2004.

Some Researchers Find Other Factors May Trigger Consumer Bankruptcies and that Credit Cards Role Varied

Some academics, consumer advocacy groups, and others have indicated that the rise in consumer bankruptcy filings has occurred because the normal life events that reduce incomes or increase expenses for households have more serious effects today. Events that can reduce household incomes include job losses, pay cuts, or conversion of full-time positions to part-time work. Medical emergencies can result in increased household expenses and debts. Divorces can both reduce income and increase expenses. One researcher explained that, while households have faced the same kinds of risks for generations, the likelihood of these types of life events occurring has increased. This researcher's studies noted that the likelihood of job loss or financial distress arising from medical problems and the risk of divorce have all increased. Furthermore, more households send all adults into the workforce, and, while this increases their income, it also doubles their total risk exposure, which increases their likelihood of having to file for bankruptcy. According to this researcher, about 94 percent of families who filed for bankruptcy would qualify as middle class.[9]

Although many of the people who file for bankruptcy have considerable credit card debt, those researchers that asserted that life events were the primary explanation for filings noted that the role played by credit cards varied. According to one of these researchers, individuals who have filed for bankruptcy with outstanding credit card debt could be classified into three groups:

- Those who had built up household debts, including substantial credit card balances, but filed for bankruptcy after experiencing a life event that adversely affected their expenses or incomes such that they could not meet their obligations.

- Those who experienced a life event that adversely affected their expenses or incomes, and increased their usage of credit cards to avoid falling behind on other secured debt payments (such as mortgage debt), but who ultimately failed to recover and filed for bankruptcy.

- Those with very little credit card debt who filed for bankruptcy when they could no longer make payments on their secured debt. This represented the smallest category of people filing for bankruptcy.

---

[9]Elizabeth Warren, Leo Gottlieb Professor of Law, Harvard Law School, "The Growing Threat to Middle Class Families," *Brooklyn Law Review*, (April 2003).

Factors Contributing to the Profitability of Credit Card Issuers

Various factors help to explain why banks that focus on credit card lending generally have higher profitability than other lenders. The major source of income for credit card issuers comes from interest they earn from their cardholders who carry balances—that is, do not payoff the entire outstanding balance when due. One factor that contributes to the high profitability of credit card operations is that the average interest rates charged on credit cards are generally higher than rates charged on other types of lending. Rates charged on credit cards are generally the highest because they are extensions of credit that are not secured by any collateral from the borrower. Unlike credit cards, most other types of consumer lending involve the extension of a fixed amount of credit under fixed terms of repayment (i.e., the borrower must repay an established amount of principal, plus interest each month) and are collateralized—such as loans for cars, under which the lender can repossess the car in the event the borrower does not make the scheduled loan payments. Similarly, mortgage loans that allow borrowers to purchase homes are secured by the underlying house. Loans with collateral and fixed repayment terms pose less risk of loss, and thus lenders can charge less interest on such loans. In contrast, credit card loans, which are unsecured, available to large and heterogeneous populations, and can be repaid on flexible terms at the cardholders' convenience, present greater risks and have commensurately higher interest rates.

As shown in figure 27, data from the Federal Reserve shows that average interest rates charged on credit cards were generally higher than interest rates charged on car loans and personal loans. Similarly, average interest rates charged on corporate loans are also generally lower than credit cards, with the best business customers often paying the prime rate, which averaged 6.19 percent during 2005.

Figure 27: Average Credit Card, Car Loans and Personal Loan Interest Rates

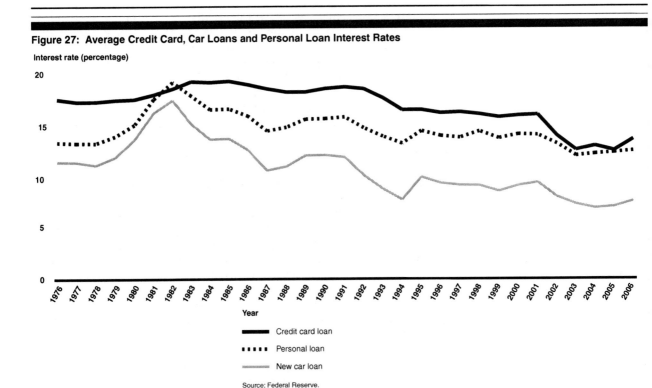

Source: Federal Reserve.

Moreover, many card issuers have increasingly begun setting the interest rates they charge their cardholders using variable rates that change as a specified market index rate, such as the prime rate, changes. This allows credit card issuers' interest revenues to rise as their cost of funding rises during times when market interest rates are increasing. Of the most popular cards issued by the largest card issuers between 2004 and 2005 that we analyzed, more than 90 percent had variable rates that changed according to an index rate. For example, the rate that the cardholder would pay on these large issuer cards was determined by adding between 6 and 8 percent to the current prime rate, with a new rate being calculated monthly.

As a result of the higher interest charges assessed on cards and variable rate pricing, banks that focus on credit card lending had the highest net interest margin compared with other types of lenders. The net interest income of a bank is the difference between what it has earned on its interest-bearing assets, including the balances on credit cards it has issued and the amounts loaned out as part of any other lending activities, and its interest expenses. To compare across banks, analysts calculate net interest margins, which express each banks' net interest income as a percentage of interest-bearing assets. The Federal Deposit Insurance Corporation (FDIC) aggregates data for a group of all federally insured banks that focus on credit card lending, which it defines as those with more than 50 percent of managed assets engaged in credit card operations; in 2005, FDIC identified 33 banks with at least this much credit card lending activity. As shown in figure 28, the net interest margin of all credit card banks, which averaged more than 8 percent, was about two to three times as high as other consumer and mortgage lending activities in 2005. Five of the six largest issuers reported to us that their average net interest margin in 2005 was even higher, at 9 percent.

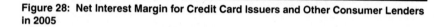

Figure 28: Net Interest Margin for Credit Card Issuers and Other Consumer Lenders in 2005

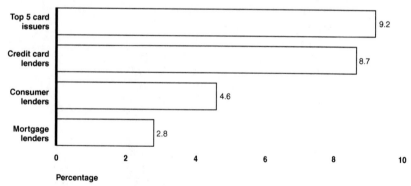

Source: GAO analysis of public financial statements of the five largest credit card issuers.

Credit Card Operations Also Have Higher Rates of Loan Losses and Operating Expenses

Although profitable, credit card operations generally experience higher charge-off rates and operating expenses than those of other types of lending. Because these loans are generally unsecured, meaning the borrower will not generally immediately lose an asset—such as a car or house—if payments are not made, borrowers may be more likely to cease making payments on their credit cards if they become financially distressed than they would for other types of credit. As a result, the rate of losses that credit card issuers experience on credit cards is higher than that incurred on other types of credit. Under bank regulatory accounting practices, banks must write off the principal balance outstanding on any loan when it is determined that the bank is unlikely to collect on the debt. For credit cards, this means that banks must deduct, as a loan loss from their income, the amount of balance outstanding on any credit card accounts for which either no payments have been made within the last 180 days or the bank has received notice that the cardholder has filed for bankruptcy. This procedure is called charging the debt off. Card issuers have much higher charge-off rates compared to other consumer lending businesses as shown in figure 29.

Figure 29: Charge-off Rates for Credit Card and Other Consumer Lenders, 2004 to 2005

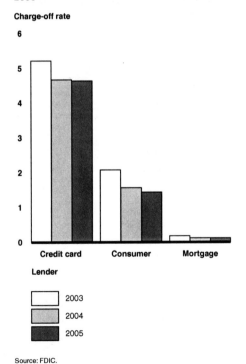

Charge-off rate

Lender

- 2003
- 2004
- 2005

Source: FDIC.

The largest credit card issuers also reported similarly high charge-off rates for their credit card operations. As shown in figure 30, five of the top six credit card issuers that we obtained data from reported that their average charge-off rate was higher than 5.5 percent between 2003 and 2005, well above other consumer lenders' average net charge-off rate of 1.44 percent.

Figure 30: Charge-off Rates for the Top 5 Credit Card Issuers, 2003 to 2005

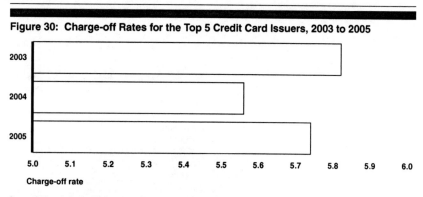

Source: GAO analysis of public financial statements of the five largest credit card issuers.

Credit card issuers also incur higher operating expenses compared with other consumer lenders. Operating expense is another one of the largest cost items for card issuers and, according to a credit card industry research firm, accounts for approximately 37 percent of total expenses in 2005. The operating expenses of a credit card issuer include staffing and the information technology costs that are incurred to maintain cardholders' accounts. Operating expense as a proportion of total assets for credit card lending is higher because offering credit cards often involves various activities that other lending activities do not. For example, issuers often incur significant expenses in postage and other marketing costs as part of soliciting new customers. In addition, some credit cards now provide rewards and loyalty programs that allow cardholders to earn rewards such as free airline tickets, discounts on merchandise, or cash back on their accounts, which are not generally expenses associated with other types of lending. Credit card operating expense burden also may be higher because issuers must service a large number of relatively small accounts. For example, the six large card issuers that we surveyed reported that they each had an average of 30 million credit card accounts, the average outstanding balance on these accounts was about $2,500, and 48 percent of accounts did not revolve balances in 2005.

As a result, the average operating expense, as a percentage of total assets for banks, that focus on credit card lending averaged over 9 percent in 2005, as shown in figure 31, which was well above the 3.44 percent average for other consumer lenders. The largest issuers operating expenses may not be as high as all banks that focus on credit card lending because their larger operations give them some cost advantages from economies of scale. For example, they may be able to pay lower postage rates by being able to segregate the mailings of account statements to their cardholders by zip code, thus qualifying for bulk-rate discounts.

Figure 31: Operating Expense as Percentage of Total Assets for Various Types of Lenders in 2005

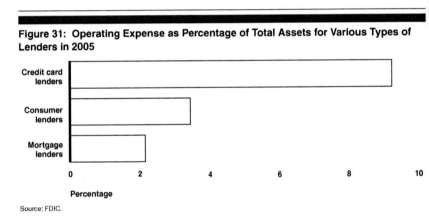

Source: FDIC.

Another reason that the banks that issue credit cards are more profitable than other types of lenders is that they earn greater percentage of revenues from noninterest sources, including fees, than lenders that focus more on other types of consumer lending. As shown in figure 32, FDIC data indicates that the ratio of noninterest revenues to assets—an indicator of noninterest income generated from outstanding credit loans—is about 10 percent for the banks that focus on credit card lending, compared with less than 2.8 percent for other lenders.

Figure 32: Non-Interest Revenue as Percentage of Their Assets for Card Lenders and Other Consumer Lenders

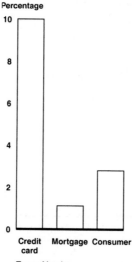

Source: GAO analysis of FDIC data.

Effect of Penalty Interest and Fees on Credit Card Issuer Profitability

Although penalty interest and fees apparently have increased, their effect on issuer profitability may not be as great as other factors. For example, while more cardholders appeared to be paying default rates of interest on their cards, issuers have not been experiencing greater profitability from interest revenues. According to our analysis of FDIC Quarterly Banking Profile data, the revenues that credit card issuers earn from interest generally have been stable over the last 18 years.[1] As shown in figure 33, net interest margin for all banks that focused on credit card lending has ranged between 7.4 percent and 9.6 percent since 1987. Similarly, according to the data that five of the top six issuers provided to us, their net interest margins have been relatively stable between 2003 and 2005, ranging from 9.2 percent to 9.6 percent during this period.

[1]The Quarterly Banking Profile is issued by the FDIC and provides a comprehensive summary of financial results for all FDIC-insured institutions. This report card on industry status and performance includes written analyses, graphs, and statistical tables.

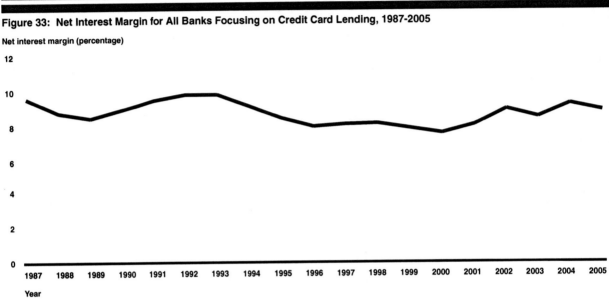

Figure 33: Net Interest Margin for All Banks Focusing on Credit Card Lending, 1987-2005

Net interest margin (percentage)

Year

Source: FDIC.

These data suggest that increases in penalty interest assessments could be offsetting decreases in interest revenues from other cardholders. During the last few years, card issuers have competed vigorously for market share. In doing so, they frequently have offered cards to new cardholders that feature low interest rates—including zero percent for temporary introductory periods, usually 8 months—either for purchases or sometimes for balances transferred from other cards. The extent to which cardholders now are paying such rates is not known, but the six largest issuers reported to us that the proportion of their cardholders paying interest rates below 5 percent—which could be cardholders enjoying temporarily low introductory rates—represented about 7 percent of their cardholders between 2003 and 2005. To the extent that card issuers have been receiving lower interest as the result of these marketing efforts, such declines could be masking the effect of increasing amounts of penalty interest on their overall interest revenues.

Although revenues from penalty fees have grown, their effect on overall issuer profitability is less than the effect of income from interest or other factors. For example, we obtained information from a Federal Reserve

Bank researcher with data from one of the credit card industry surveys that illustrated that the issuers' cost of funds may be a more significant factor for their profitability lately. Banks generally obtain the funds they use to lend to others through their operations from various sources, such as checking or savings deposits, income on other investments, or borrowing from other banks or creditors. The average rate of interest they pay on these funding sources represents their cost of funds. As shown in table 4 below, the total cost of funds (for $100 in credit card balances outstanding) for the credit card banks included in this survey declined from $8.98 in 1990 to a low of $2.00 in 2004—a decrease of 78 percent. Because card issuers' net interest income generally represents a much higher percentage of revenues than does income from penalty fees, its impact on issuers' overall profitability is greater; thus the reduction in the cost of funds likely contributed significantly to the general rise in credit card banks' profitability over this time.

Table 4: Revenues and Profits of Credit Card Issuers in Card Industry Directory per $100 of Credit Card Assets

Revenues and profits	1990	2004	Percent change
Interest revenues	$16.42	$12.45	-24%
Cost of funds	8.98	2.00	-78
Net interest income	7.44	10.45	40
Interchange fee revenues	2.15	2.87	33
Penalty fee revenues	0.69	1.40	103
Annual fee revenues	1.25	0.42	-66
Other revenues	0.18	0.87	383
Total revenue from operations	11.71	16.01	37
Other expenses	8.17	10.41	27
Taxes	1.23	1.99	62
Net income	2.30	3.61	57

Source: GAO Analysis of Card Industry Directory data.

Although card issuer revenues from penalty fees have been increasing since the 1980s, they remain a small portion of overall revenues. As shown in table 4 above, our analysis of the card issuer data obtained from the Federal Reserve indicated that the amount of revenues that issuers collected from penalty fees for every $100 in credit card balances outstanding climbed from 69 cents to $1.40 between 1990 and 2004—an increase of 103 percent. During this same period, net interest income collected per $100 in card balances outstanding grew from $7.44 to $10.45—an increase of about 41 percent. However, the relative size of each of these two sources of income indicates that interest income is between 7 to 8 times more important to issuer revenues than penalty fee income is in 2004. Furthermore, during this same time, collections of annual fees from cardholders declined from $1.25 to 42 cents per every $100 in card balances—which means that the total of annual and penalty fees in 2004 is about the same as in 1990 and that this decline may also be offsetting the increased revenues from penalty fees.

Comments from the Federal Reserve Board

BOARD OF GOVERNORS
OF THE
FEDERAL RESERVE SYSTEM
WASHINGTON, D. C. 20551

SANDRA F. BRAUNSTEIN
DIRECTOR
DIVISION OF CONSUMER
AND COMMUNITY AFFAIRS

August 23, 2006

Mr. David G. Wood
Director, Financial Markets and Community
    Investment
U.S. Government Accountability Office
441 G Street, NW
Washington, DC 20548

Dear Mr. Wood:

Thank you for the opportunity to comment on the GAO's draft report entitled Credit Cards: Increased Complexity in Rates and Fees Heightens Need for More Effective Disclosures to Consumers. As the report notes, the Federal Reserve Board has commenced a comprehensive rulemaking to review the Truth in Lending Act (TILA) rules for open-end (revolving) credit, including credit card accounts. The primary goal of the review is to improve the effectiveness and usefulness of consumer disclosures and the substantive protections provided under the Board's Regulation Z, which implements TILA. To ensure that consumers get timely information in a readable form, the Board is studying alternatives for improving both the content and format of disclosures, including revising the model forms published by the Board.

The draft GAO report specifically recommends that the Board revise credit card disclosures to emphasize more clearly the account terms that can significantly affect cardholder costs, such as default or other penalty pricing rates. We agree that increased complexity in credit card pricing has added to the complexity of the disclosures. To help address this, the Board has invited public comment on ways in which the disclosures required under Regulation Z can be made more meaningful to consumers. The Board is conducting extensive consumer testing to determine what information is most important to consumers, when that information is most useful, what language and formats work best, and how disclosures can be simplified, prioritized, and organized to reduce complexity and information overload. To that end, the Board has hired design consultants to assist in developing model disclosures that are most likely to be effective in communicating information to consumers. Importantly, the Board also plans to use consumer testing to assist in developing model disclosure forms. Based on this review and testing, the Board will revise Regulation Z and, if appropriate, develop suggested statutory changes for congressional consideration.

Mr. David G. Wood
Page 2

The Board's staff has provided technical comments on the draft GAO report separately. We appreciate the efforts of your staff to respond to our comments.

Sincerely,

c: Cody Goebel, Assistant Director, GAO

GAO Contact and Staff Acknowledgments

GAO Contact

Dave Wood (202) 512-8678

Staff Acknowledgments

In addition to those named above, Cody Goebel, Assistant Director; Jon Altshul; Rachel DeMarcus; Kate Magdelena Gonzalez; Christine Houle; Christine Kuduk; Marc Molino; Akiko Ohnuma; Carl Ramirez; Omyra Ramsingh; Barbara Roesmann; Kathryn Supinski; Richard Vagnoni; Anita Visser; and Monica Wolford made key contributions to this report.

GAO's Mission	The Government Accountability Office, the audit, evaluation and investigative arm of Congress, exists to support Congress in meeting its constitutional responsibilities and to help improve the performance and accountability of the federal government for the American people. GAO examines the use of public funds; evaluates federal programs and policies; and provides analyses, recommendations, and other assistance to help Congress make informed oversight, policy, and funding decisions. GAO's commitment to good government is reflected in its core values of accountability, integrity, and reliability.
Obtaining Copies of GAO Reports and Testimony	The fastest and easiest way to obtain copies of GAO documents at no cost is through GAO's Web site (www.gao.gov). Each weekday, GAO posts newly released reports, testimony, and correspondence on its Web site. To have GAO e-mail you a list of newly posted products every afternoon, go to www.gao.gov and select "Subscribe to Updates."
Order by Mail or Phone	The first copy of each printed report is free. Additional copies are $2 each. A check or money order should be made out to the Superintendent of Documents. GAO also accepts VISA and Mastercard. Orders for 100 or more copies mailed to a single address are discounted 25 percent. Orders should be sent to:
	U.S. Government Accountability Office 441 G Street NW, Room LM Washington, D.C. 20548

	To order by Phone: Voice: (202) 512-6000
	                      TDD: (202) 512-2537
	                      Fax: (202) 512-6061

To Report Fraud, Waste, and Abuse in Federal Programs	Contact: Web site: www.gao.gov/fraudnet/fraudnet.htm E-mail: fraudnet@gao.gov Automated answering system: (800) 424-5454 or (202) 512-7470
Congressional Relations	Gloria Jarmon, Managing Director, JarmonG@gao.gov (202) 512-4400 U.S. Government Accountability Office, 441 G Street NW, Room 7125 Washington, D.C. 20548
Public Affairs	Paul Anderson, Managing Director, AndersonP1@gao.gov (202) 512-4800 U.S. Government Accountability Office, 441 G Street NW, Room 7149 Washington, D.C. 20548

LaVergne, TN USA
13 March 2011
219935LV00005B/99/P